Human Reproduction

HEALTH AND HYGIENE

Human Reproduction

HEALTH AND HYGIENE

New Edition

THOMAS H. KNEPP

Preface by Richard V. Lee, M.D.

Carbondale and Edwardsville

SOUTHERN ILLINOIS UNIVERSITY PRESS

FEFFER & SIMONS, INC.

London and Amsterdam

PREFACE

SEX EDUCATION is a continuing process for parents, for instructors, and certainly for the individual as he or she grows toward that mystical event sometimes called "maturity." Its importance is far too great to be delegated by default to the peer group of a child or adolescent.

As a physician in a college setting, it is both easy and painful to attest to the fact that many entering students do bring with them conceptions about themselves based entirely on ignorance; all too often such conceptions are the harbingers of serious difficulty in the young adult. To relegate this aspect of education to television, movies, or pulp fiction is to invite both personal and social disaster.

Ideally construed, sexual expression in the human is much more than satisfaction of primitive impulses or curiosity. It is, or should be, the noblest expression of love and true affection between individuals who have agreed to share all life's experiences together in dignity, with resolve. In our society such a relationship exists only in marriage, in which such a public declaration is made.

A person is an animal by accident, a man or woman by choice. It behooves us as educators, parents, and sympathetic human beings to constantly strive to present factual information in proper context, in order that value judgments will be rational and solid.

In writing this book, the author has commendably presented factual material accurately, interestingly, and concisely. The book is not intended to be a compendium, but should serve both as an excellent textual resource as well as a basic platform from which to lead intelligent discussion.

Richard V. Lee, M.D.
University Director of Health Services

Southern Illinois University
February 20, 1967

ACKNOWLEDGMENTS

I am indebted to certain individuals who were kind enough to read my manuscript and make corrections. My gratitude, therefore, is expressed to L. W. Hunsicker, M.D., Mary T. Hunsicker, M.D., M. J. Leitner, M.D., and to my daughter, Mary E. Knepp, M.D.

My wife, Mildred, read the manuscript and made suggestions for improvement. To all these people I wish to extend my thanks and appreciation.

Thomas H. Knepp

Stroudsburg, Pennsylvania
January 31, 1967

CONTENTS

Preface   v

Acknowledgments   vii

1 Puberty and Adolescence   3

2 The Male Reproductive System   6

3 The Female Reproductive System   17

4 Coitus   34

5 Human Embryology   41

6 Pregnancy   48

7 Birth   53

8 Multiple Birth, Sex Determination, and
   Rh Factor   61

9 Venereal Disease   68

   Glossary   79

   Suggested Reading List   89

   References   93

   Index   97

Human Reproduction
HEALTH AND HYGIENE

1. Puberty and Adolescence

One of the most important parts of the human body is the reproductive system, but many young people have had little instruction about its anatomy and physiology. They have a healthy curiosity about their bodily changes, and with this curiosity come questions concerning reproduction as the body matures and gets ready to fulfill its function of producing human life.

As boys and girls grow older their body chemistry changes, and they enter the stage of life known as *puberty* [pu'ber-te]. Prior to puberty the body develops and grows under the control of the *hypophysis* [hi-pof'ĭ-sis], the master gland located at the base of the brain. (Another name for the hypophysis is the *pituitary* [pĭ-tu'ĭ-tār'e], but hypophysis is the preferred technical term.) The chemical substances, called *hormones* [hor'mōnz], produced by the hypophysis affect various parts of the body, including the sex glands. The male sex glands are the *testes* [tes'tēz], or *testicles* [tes'tĭ-k'lz], which produce the *spermatozoa* [sper'mah-to-zo'ah], often called *sperm*, or male sex cells. The female sex glands are the *ovaries* [o'vah-rez], which produce the *ova* [o'vah], or egg cells. The sex glands also produce their own specific hormones, which have a pronounced effect upon the male and female bodies.

Hormones produced by the testes have these effects on the male: he becomes more muscular, hair appears

4

in his armpits and *pubic* [pu'bik] region (the extreme lower portion of the front of the body), his beard develops, and his voice deepens as the vocal cords increase in size.

In the girl's body, hormones produced by the ovaries cause the hips to widen, the breasts to grow, and the body in general to become more rounded as fat is deposited under the skin. Hair grows in the armpits and in the pubic region, and *menstruation* [men'strooa'shun] begins.

The pubic-hair pattern of the female is different from that of the male. In the former, the hair forms a V with a rather straight line across the pubic region. The pubic hair of males is in the shape of an inverted V (∧), with a rather indefinite upper limit as the pattern ascends the abdomen and may even fuse with the hair of the chest. In both sexes there are normal variations among individuals from the typical patterns. Relatively few women have hair on their chest, although there are some who have scattered hair on the breasts.

These bodily changes are called secondary sex characteristics because they are not directly concerned with reproduction. The primary sex characteristics, those which relate directly to the process of reproduction, will be discussed in the next two chapters.

The onset of puberty varies in individuals of the same sex. Girls may enter puberty as early as ten, or the onset may be delayed until sixteen or seventeen years of age. Boys begin puberty about thirteen, although for some it may be earlier or may not begin until the middle-teen years. Variations in the onset of puberty are normal, indicating that humans are not all alike.

During the teen years boys' and girls' bodies and minds grow and mature as they develop into young men and young women. This is the period of life known as *adolescence* [ad′o-les′ens]. This period is a challenge to every boy and girl, as the years are filled with new experiences for the young men and women approaching adulthood.

2. The Male Reproductive System

External System

The reproductive system of the male includes both external and internal organs, or *genitalia* [jen′ĭ-ta′le-ah]. First, we will discuss the external ones, the *penis* [pe′nis]—from Latin, meaning "tail"—and the *scrotum* [skro′tum]—from Latin, meaning "bag." At birth a boy has a large, flabby scrotum and a rather small penis. When puberty begins the penis and scrotum grow larger until they reach adult size.

Penis

As early as the seventh week of *embryonic* [em′bre-on′ik] *life*—seven weeks after the egg is fertilized—the beginning of the penis is evident in a pointed structure called a *genital tubercle* [jen′ĭ-tal tu′ber-k'l]. As development of the male *embryo* [em-bre-o]—the unborn child—continues, the penis takes form. At birth it is ready to function in the discharge of urine from the bladder.

The penis is a cylindrical-shaped organ that hangs from the extreme lower part of the front of the body. It rests somewhat on the scrotum and consists of three parts, the *body, glans* [glanz], and *prepuce* [pre′pūs]. The cylindrical portion of the penis is called the body, or shaft. At the free end there is an enlarged, smooth glans, or head, which is covered by the prepuce, sometimes called the *foreskin,* a double fold of skin, which usually fits loosely over the glans.

The edge of the glans contains a number of very sensitive nerve endings called *genital corpuscles* [kor'-pus'lz]; these are not found at any other place in the male reproductive system. During sexual relations they stimulate excitement in the male.

Just back of the glans there are glands (notice the difference in spelling of glans and glands) which produce a cheesy secretion called *smegma* [smeg'mah]— from the Greek word for "soap." If smegma is left to accumulate under the prepuce it irritates adjacent tissue, causing discomfort. The odor is also objectionable. As a matter of body cleanliness it is necessary that the prepuce be loose enough so it can be drawn back and the glans washed with soap and water. In some boys the prepuce covers the glans so tightly that it is surgically removed by a minor operation called *circumcision* [ser'kum-sizh'un]. Today most boys are circumcised a few days after they are born for hygienic or religious reasons.

The body of the penis is composed of three masses of spongy tissue which run the length of the penis. When the male is sexually excited, blood flows into the spongy tissue faster than it drains away. The blood presses upon the tissue walls, causing the penis to become hard and erect. It is then in a state of *erection* [e-rek'shun], and in this condition can be inserted into the *vagina* [vah-ji'nah] of the female in the act of *coitus* [ko'i-tus], or *sexual intercourse*. After the *semen* [se'men]—sperm and the fluid in which they swim— has been discharged the blood drains out of the spongy tissue, and the penis becomes soft again.

The *urethra* [u-re'thrah] is a tube which runs through the penis on the underside from the bladder and is the outlet for the evacuation of urine. When the penis is in erection the flow of urine is blocked off, so that at the proper moment semen may be discharged through the tube. Therefore, the urethra of the male serves a double purpose—it carries urine and semen out of the body but not at the same time.

Scrotum

During the tenth to twelfth week of development two structures in the embryo called *genital swellings* grow large and fuse to form the scrotum; the area of fusion is externally evident thereafter. Internally the scrotum is divided into two compartments, one for each testis. The outer layer of the skin has muscles which cause the scrotum to be wrinkled, and under the influence of cold these muscles contract and cause the scrotum to become smaller and to fit more tightly into the crotch. In a warm environment the muscles relax, and the scrotum drops away from the crotch and becomes more baglike. In this way the testes are kept at a constant temperature.

Male animals have a variety of scrotal patterns. The scrotum of a dog is very close to the body; a tomcat's scrotum can hardly be seen. That of a stallion is slightly saclike. In a bull the scrotum is a long, pouch-like structure, which hangs down between the hind legs. Bull elephants and bull whales have no scrotum.

Internal System

The principal internal reproductive organs of the human male are the testis, the *epididymis* [ep′ĭ-did′ĭ-mis], the *vas deferens* [vas def′er-enz], and the *prostate* [pros′tāt] *gland*—all connected and interrelated. There is only one prostate gland, but one of each of the other three is found on both the left and the right sides of the body.

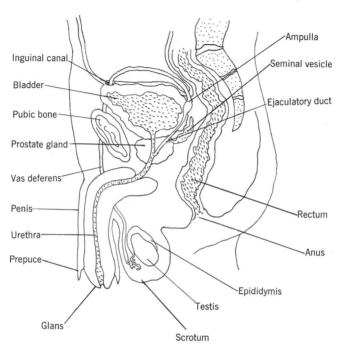

Inguinal canal

Bladder

Pubic bone

Prostate gland

Vas deferens

Penis

Urethra

Prepuce

Glans

Scrotum

Testis

Epididymis

Anus

Rectum

Ejaculatory duct

Seminal vesicle

Ampulla

1. *Male urogenital organs (from left side). The sperm mature in the seminiferous tubules within the testis and are carried to the epididymis which doubles back on itself and becomes the vas deferens as it passes out of the scrotum. The vas deferens ascends internally (behind the penis in the above view), joins the excretory duct from the seminal vesicle to form the ejaculatory duct, which crosses the prostate gland and empties into the upper part of the urethra, shown descending from the bladder.*

Testes

In human embryos that are ¼ inch long (about five weeks) there are already two germinal ridges of tissue from which there will eventually develop either the testes or the ovaries. By the time the embryo is ½ inch long (about six weeks) the cells of these ridges begin to show indications of being testicular cells, if the child is to be a male. As the embryo continues to grow, the testes are formed inside the body near the kidneys. At about thirty-two weeks of *fetal* [fe'tal] *life* — during the early weeks the developing baby is referred to as an embryo, but from eight weeks till birth it is called a *fetus* [fe'tus] — the testes descend into the scrotum.

After each testis has descended into the scrotum the pathway narrows into a structure known as the *inguinal* [ing'gwĭ-nal] *canal.* Sometimes this canal does not close as it should, and part of the intestine may descend through the canal into the scrotum, causing an *inguinal hernia* [her'ne-ah]. Surgical repair of this type of hernia is almost always possible. In some animals, such as rodents and bats, the inguinal canal remains open, with the testes descending periodically into the scrotum during breeding season.

Sometimes in man the testes fail to move from inside the body into the scrotum. This condition is known as *cryptorchidism* [krip-tor'kĭ-dizm] — from the Greek for "hidden testis" — a condition which is sometimes associated with *sterility* [ste-ril'ĭ-te] — inability to produce young. Cryptorchidism is found in approximately 20 out of 1000 boys below the age of fourteen but in only 2 out of 1000 adult men. This indicates that in many males the testes descend later — undescended testes have been known to descend of their own accord as late as the eighteenth year. In 15 per cent to 20 per cent of all cases the cryptorchidism involves both testes. Where the condition exists only on one side, the right testis is involved twice as frequently as the left one. Incomplete descent after puberty results in withering away of tissues within the testis and subsequent cessation of sperm formation; the degree of atrophy increases with age. The cryptorchid testis is more likely to be injured and subject to cancer than the normal one. Men with both testes undescended are sterile and frequently are in a similar condition to that of a *eunuch* [u'nuk]—a male who has had his testes removed—indicating that certain cells of the testes have failed to produce the hormone which is responsible for male characteristics.

The testis is somewhat egg-shaped being about 1½ inches long and about 1 inch wide. In most men the left testis hangs a little lower than the right one. The testis is enclosed in a rather thick, fibrous cover, which dips into the interior of the organ dividing it into lobes.

Internally the testis is made up of two types of tissue—the *seminiferous tubules* [se'mĭ-nif'er-us tu'-būlz], which produce sperm and the *interstitial* [in'ter-stish'al] *cells*, which produce hormones.

Seminiferous Tubules Each testis contains many seminiferous tubules tightly coiled within the lobes into which the testis is divided—individual tubules may be 1 to 2 feet in length. Internally each tubule is lined with many male sex cells, which by a maturing process called *spermatogenesis* [sper'mah-to-jen'e-sis] become sperm cells. The sperm cell of a human male is about $\frac{1}{400}$ inch long and consists of an expanded head, a narrow neck, a body, and a long tail. After puberty sperm are produced continually in almost unbelievable numbers, and as they mature they are set free in the center cavity of the tubule. Within the tubule there are also *Sertoli* (named for Enrico Sertoli, 1842–1910, an Italian histologist—one who studies tissue), or *sustentacular* [sus'ten-tak'u-lar], *cells*, to which sperm may attach to obtain nourishment.

Interstitial Cells The interstitial, or *Leydig*

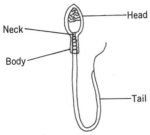

2. *Enlarged view of a sperm, the male sex cell, produced in the seminiferous tubules of the testis. The expanded head carries the chromosome load and, upon fertilization, unites with the nucleus of the egg cell.*

3. *Duct system of the right testis, showing the lobes into which the testis is divided. The seminiferous tubules come together to form the rete, or network, of the testis; the rete opens into the epididymis.*

(named for Franz Leydig, a German zoologist, 1821–1908), cells are located between the tubules and secrete hormones, one of which is called *androgen* [an′dro-jen]. (Androgen and *estrogen* [es′tro-jen] are singular rather than plural here because the terms are used in their generic sense.) The most important androgenic hormone is *testosterone* [tes-tos′ter-ōn], which is responsible for the development of the secondary sex organs—the prostate and *seminal vesicles* [sem′ĭ-nal ves′ĭ-k'ls] and their secretions—and for the appearance of the secondary sex characteristics. (Only part of the androgenic substances circulating in a man are produced in the testes. It is interesting to note that both men and women secrete androgen and estrogen—the female hormone—but in different amounts.)

Androgen is found in all male vertebrates and is

responsible for such male characteristics as the form of the male body—such as the bullneck of the domestic bull and bull bison, the lower pitch of the human-male voice, the distribution of male body hair, the comb of the rooster, the clasping fingers of the male frog, and the color changes of certain male fishes. In animals some of these characteristics appear only during the breeding season.

The existence of the male sex hormone in the testes is experimentally proved by the complete removal of the testes, a process called *castration* [kas-tra′shun]— castrated humans are called eunuchs. When this is done before puberty the human male does not develop the obvious male sex characteristics—very little hair appears on the face, the voice fails to deepen, the skin is soft and pale, the growth and distribution of body hair are adversely affected, the shoulders do not fill out, and the bones of the upper and lower extremities grow longer than usual. If castration is effected after the human male becomes an adult, the outward appearance of the man is little, if any, changed. Studies made in Germany of men who were castrated by wounds received in World War I substantiate this statement.

For centuries man has been castrating his domestic animals to make them tamer, fatter, or tastier. Castration has an effect on sex behavior, especially among nonhumans. After castration guinea pigs and some domestic animals show an interest in the female, but later this interest diminishes; no production of sex cells is possible if the testes are removed. However, it should be pointed out that in noncastrated males who are sterile sex hormones may still be produced, for although eunuchs are sterile not all sterile males are eunuchs.

Epididymis and Vas Deferens

The seminiferous tubules from the lobes of the testis come together to form 10 to 15 ducts (tubes) which carry the sperm to a highly coiled structure called the epididymis, located behind and loosely attached to the testis. The epididymis is about 2 inches long and ¼ inch wide, but contains a tube 18 to 20 feet long. The coils are lined with cilia which propel the sperm along. At the bottom of the testis the epididymis doubles back on itself, then becomes the vas deferens, which passes out of the scrotum, ascends internally through the lower pelvic region, then descends toward the urethra where it joins the vas deferens from the other side. Closely packed sperm are not entirely capable of self-movement in the tubules, epididymis, and vas deferens, but the cilia of the epididymis and contractions of the vas deferens propel them to the distant end of the vas deferens. There an enlargement called the *ampulla* [am-pul′lah]—from Latin, meaning "jug"—acts as a reservoir for the collected sperm.

Accessory Sex Glands

We now turn to the back of the bladder to study the accessory sex glands. Low down on each side of the bladder is a somewhat coiled and branched outgrowth of the vas deferens called the seminal vesicle. This produces a sticky secretion which is discharged with the sperm from the vas deferens through the *ejaculatory* [e-jak′u-lah-to′re] *duct* which is common to both the seminal vesicle and the vas deferens.

Prostate Gland

The ejaculatory duct crosses the upper part of an-

other accessory sex gland, the prostate, which surrounds the neck of the bladder and the beginning of
the urethra. (Note that the spelling is prostate, *not*
prostrate. The latter word means to "lie flat.") The
prostate is shaped somewhat like a strawberry, about
1½ inches by 1¼ inches in size. It is composed of
muscular and glandular tissue. The glandular portion
produces a milky, alkaline secretion. At the climax of
the sex act the muscular tissue of the prostate forces
this secretion out through a network of 20 to 30 small
ducts which open as pores into the upper part of the
urethra. Here the secretion becomes mixed with sperm
and the secretion of the seminal vesicles which have
entered the urethra through the ejaculatory duct. This
mixture of sperm and the secretions from the seminal
vesicles and the prostate is called semen, a somewhat
thick, whitish, and slightly stringy discharge with a
characteristic odor. The discharge of semen is called
an *emission* [e-mish'un]. An emission may contain
from 200,000,000 to 300,000,000 sperm cells in the
approximately 1 teaspoon of semen.

From an anatomical standpoint the prostate is rather
badly located, as it surrounds the neck of the bladder.
In older men it has a tendency to enlarge, and it may
gradually reduce the opening of the bladder to the
urethra and make urination difficult.

Nocturnal Emissions

Once puberty begins the testes produce a continual supply of sperm to fill the tubules, epididymis, and
vas deferens. These accumulated sperm may be discharged during sleep; the penis becomes erect and
firm, and semen spurts from it. This is called a *nocturnal* [nok-tur'nal] *emission*, or *wet dream* when accom-

panied by a vivid dream of some sexual experience.

Nocturnal emissions are the result of normal body activity over which the individual has no control. They do not occur at regular intervals. They may be spaced months apart, or they may occur on several successive nights, especially if a boy becomes sexually aroused by frequent petting. Nocturnal emissions are as normal a bodily function as the elimination of waste materials and are not harmful. Everyone who lives a healthy, normal life need not worry about the regular functions of his body. If there is concern about any part of the body, a physician should be consulted.

3.   The Female Reproductive System

Many systems of the human body are the same, or very similar, in both sexes—for example, the muscular, circulatory, digestive, and skeletal systems. However, the reproductive systems are different, and because of childbearing the *pelvis* [pel′vis] assumes a greater importance in connection with the female reproductive system. In young boys and girls each hipbone is composed of three separate parts, but by adulthood these bones have fused at the socket of the hipbone into which the thighbone fits. The pelvic girdle is formed by the left and right hipbones which are strongly bound to each other and to bones of the vertebral column by ligaments. Because of the function of childbearing the hipbones of the female are set farther apart than those of the male, and the bones are of a different size from those of the male. The largest part of the hipbone forms the hip, the next largest makes the framework for the buttock, and the smallest, the *pubis* [pu′bis], joins the pubis of the other hipbone to form the bony structure of the extreme lower front of the body. In the female the area where the two pubic bones meet is covered by a mound of fatty tissue, named the *mons pubis* or *mons veneris* [monz ven′-er-is].

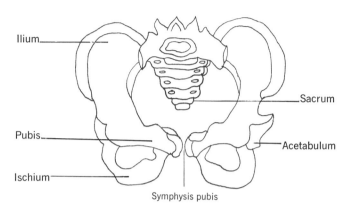

Ilium

Sacrum

Pubis

Acetabulum

Ischium

Symphysis pubis

4. *Pelvic bone structure of the female. Because of the function of childbearing the hipbones are set farther apart, the sacrum is wider and less curved toward the front of the body than in the male. The thighbone fits into the acetabulum— from Latin, meaning "vinegar cup." The ilium is roughly fan-shaped and protects the lower abdominal contents from the back and side. The ischium terminates in a rough eminence which bears the weight of the body when one sits up straight. The two pubis bones meet to form the symphysis pubis at the lower front of the body.*

External System

Most of the reproductive organs of the female are contained within the pelvis, but, as with the male, there are both external and internal parts. Our discussion will begin with the external genitalia, or *vulva* [vul′vah], which includes the *labia majora* [la′be-ah majo′ra], the *labia minora* [la′be-ah mino′ra], the *clitoris* [kli′to-ris], and the *vestibule* [ves′tĭ-būl].

Labia Majora

From the mons pubis two thick folds of skin, called the labia majora, extend down and back toward the *anus* [a′nus] where they become lost in the *perineum* [per′i-ne′um]—the area of tissue bounded by the mons pubis, the thighs, and the buttocks. The outer surface of each fold is pigmented and covered with hair; the inner surface is smooth. The labia majora are formed in the embryo from the same genital swellings which form the scrotum of the male.

Labia Minora

Inside the labia majora, toward the front of the body, there is a pair of small thin lips which are called the labia minora. These are pink or red, hairless, and are covered by a smooth, moist membrane like that on the inner surface of the labia majora. The labia minora do not extend as far back as the labia majora do, and to the front they enclose the clitoris.

Clitoris

The clitoris is formed in the embryo from the same genital tubercle which forms the penis in the male. It may be up to an inch long, and it has a body and a glans like a penis, but it does not have the urethra running through it. Most of its body is embedded in tissue; so only the glans is free. The body consists of two longitudinal masses of spongy tissue, which can become engorged with blood during sexual excitation, and the glans, as that of the penis, contains genital corpuscles—a complex of receptors and nerve endings—which are very sensitive to touch. The clitoris serves to excite the female before and during sexual intercourse.

Vestibule

The area behind the clitoris and between the labia minora is known as the vestibule into which open the urethra and the vagina. The small opening of the urethra, the tube which empties the bladder, is about an inch from the clitoris. Immediately in back of the urethra is the entrance to the vagina, which may be partially covered by a thin, perforated membrane called the *hymen* [hi′men]—the word means "membrane." The function of the hymen is not known; it generally shows variations in thickness; the perforations may show different patterns; and it may be completely absent.

Internal System

From a reproductive standpoint the internal sex organs, all located within the pelvis, are more important than the parts of the vulva just discussed. The internal organs are the vagina, the *uterus* [u′ter-us], the *fallopian* [fal-lo′pe-an] *tubes,* and the ovaries.

Vagina

The vagina is the tubular canal located between the bladder and the *rectum* [rek′tum], the lower end of the large intestine, and connects the vestibule with the *cervix* [ser′viks], the neck of the uterus or *womb* [wo͞om]. The front wall of the vagina is about 3 inches long; the back wall is about 3½ inches long. It slopes downward and forward, approximately parallel with the rectum and almost at right angles to the uterus. The muscular walls, lined with mucous membrane, are ordinarily collapsed but are separated during the *menstrual* [men′stroo-al] *flow* and intercourse, and are capable of enormous stretching during childbirth.

Uterus

The pear-shaped uterus is a thick-walled, hollow,

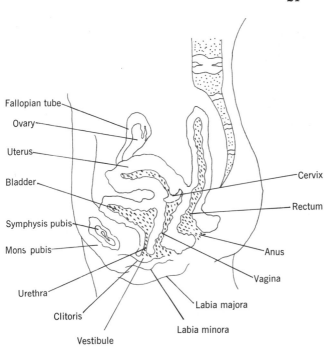

Fallopian tube

Ovary

Uterus

Bladder

Symphysis pubis

Mons pubis

Urethra

Clitoris

Vestibule

Cervix

Rectum

Anus

Vagina

Labia majora

Labia minora

5. *Female urogenital organs (from left side),
showing the relationship of the external and internal genitalia. The labia majora extend from
the mons pubis toward the anus; the clitoris is
enclosed by the labia minora. The urethra and
the vagina, located close to each other, open into
the vestibule. Note how the passage of the fetus
through the vagina during childbirth would ex-
ert pressure on both the urethra and rectum.*

muscular organ between the bladder and the rectum,
tipped slightly forward so that it overhangs the bladder. The neck (corresponding to the stem end of a
pear) is the 1 inch-long cervix which extends into the
vagina. The uterus is about 3 inches long; at the top it
measures about 2½ inches by 2 inches, and it narrows

to a diameter of about 1 inch at the cervix. The soft mucous lining of the interior cavity of the uterus is rich in blood vessels and is called the *endometrium* [en-do-me′tre-um]. Although this cavity is flattened and very small, the uterus may enlarge during pregnancy to a length of 15 inches and a width of 10 inches.

After delivery of the baby the uterus returns to nearly its original size.

The uterus is held in place by ligaments, chief among them being the broad ligament which stretches from each side of the uterus to the sidewall of the pelvis. The ovaries hang from this broad ligament, and the folds at the top of this ligament enclose the fallopian tubes, which are attached to the uterus at the broader upper end (corresponding to the bottom of a pear).

Fallopian Tubes

The fallopian tubes were named for Gabriello Fallopio, an Italian anatomist, who lived from 1523 to 1562. They are also called *uterine* [u′ter-in] *tubes* and *oviducts* [o′vĭ-dukts], but fallopian tubes is the more commonly used term. The two fallopian tubes, one attached to each side of the uterus, extend toward the ovaries, one of which is located on each side of the body. Each tube is about 4 inches long, arches over the ovary, and at the ovarian end has a trumpet-shaped and fimbriated (fringed) mouth. The *fimbriae* [fim′-bre-i] partially enwrap the ovary and possibly may assist in the process of getting the egg from the ovary into the tube. The motion of the cilia in the fallopian tube is directed toward the uterus, but it is believed that contractions in the wall of the tube actually move the egg into the uterus.

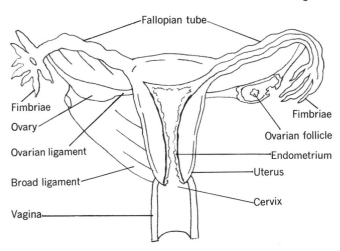

Fallopian tube

Fimbriae

Ovary

Ovarian ligament

Broad ligament

Vagina

Fimbriae

Ovarian follicle

Endometrium

Uterus

Cervix

6. *Female reproductive organs (from the back). Although the female is identical on both sides, the left side of the drawing shows the broad ligament stretching from the side of the uterus to the sidewall of the pelvis to hold the uterus in place. The ovarian ligament runs within the broad ligament and attaches the ovary to the uterine wall. The ovary is located behind and below the fallopian tube, which extends toward the ovary. The right side of the drawing shows the organs with the ligaments removed, so the ovarian follicle within the ovary can be seen. Note how close the fimbriae of the fallopian tube are to the ovary and how the fallopian tube leads into the uterus.*

Ovaries

As noted in the chapter on the male reproductive system, in human embryos that are ¼ inch long (about five weeks) there are already two ridges of tissue from which either the ovaries or the testes will develop. The cells of these ridges begin to show signs of being ovarian cells, if the child is to be a female, at about six weeks when the embryo is ½ inch long. The ovaries develop near the kidneys, migrate to the side-wall of the pelvis, and at puberty descend into their final position—one on each side of the uterus. An ovary is about 1½ inches long and about ¾ inch wide, is shaped something like an almond, and is grayish-pink in color. It is located behind and below the fallopian tube and is attached to the uterus by the ligament of the ovary; this ligament runs within the broad ligament. From the tubal extremity of the ovary (the area closest to the fimbriated end of the fallopian tube) the suspensory ligament runs to the pelvic wall.

Before we discuss the function of the ovaries we should know something about the hormones which affect this function. The anterior lobe of the hypophysis produces at least six hormones; three of these, called *gonadotropic* [gon′ah-do-trōp′ik] *hormones* because they influence the ovaries of the female and the testes of the male, are not secreted and released until puberty. These three are 1] the *follicle-stimulating hormone* (*FSH*), 2] the *luteinizing* [lu′te-in-i′zĭng] *hormone* (*LH*), and 3] the *luteotropic* [lu′te-o-tro′pĭc] *hormone* (*LTH*)—the same as *prolactin* [pro-lak′tin].

The ovary is covered by a protective layer of cells, and just under this protective cover are many *follicles* [fol′lĭ-k'lz]—special masses of cells, a number of which may ultimately develop into eggs. Unlike the continual production of sperm cells in the male after puberty, the female may have from 100,000 to 400,000 of these follicles present at birth; at puberty these move deeper into the ovaries. During a woman's reproductive years some 300 to 400 of these follicles will produce eggs which can be fertilized—each one no bigger than the period at the end of this sentence.

In each menstrual cycle the FSH stimulates the

growth of many of these follicles, and they begin an outward movement toward the surface of the ovary. Usually only one of these is "chosen" to mature; the others in both ovaries become smaller and disappear. A fluid-filled cavity develops within this one follicle, and the egg with its nucleus, protected by a mass of cells, floats in this cavity. The follicle continues to enlarge and move outward until eventually it bulges like a water blister on the surface of the ovary. (At this time the follicle is about ½ inch in diameter.) This bulging follicle is an *ovarian* [o-va're-an] *follicle,* sometimes called a *graafian* [graf'e-an] *follicle* after the celebrated Dutch physician and anatomist, Reijnier de Graaf (1641–1673).

For some as yet unknown reason this ovarian follicle ruptures, and the developing egg and fluid are forced out of the follicle; this is called *ovulation* [ov'u-la'shun]. It is generally supposed that the two ovaries alternate in producing the ripe egg every menstrual cycle. Sometimes an egg is ovulated from each ovary; if both are fertilized, *fraternal twins* are born. *Identical twins* are born when the fertilized egg divides and develops two embryos.

After ovulation the point of rupture is rapidly sealed off, and, influenced by the LH, the cells of the ovarian follicle multiply to fill the space previously occupied by the fluid. These cells contain a yellow coloring and for this reason the resulting structure is called the *corpus luteum* [kor'pus lu'teum], meaning yellow body. The corpus luteum itself produces an important hormone, *progesterone* [pro-jes'ter-ōn] for a while, but later degenerates, fills with connective tissue, loses its yellow color, and becomes an area of whitish scar tissue, called the *corpus albicans* [al'bĭ-kanz], meaning white body, on the ovary. This completes one cycle of a follicle, and at this time the FSH is starting another cycle.

The ovaries are influenced by hormones from the hypophysis, but they also secrete their own hormones. One of these is estrogen, although not all of the estrogen in a woman's body is produced by the ovaries. (As noted in the chapter on the male reproductive system, both men and women secrete androgen—the male hormone—and estrogen although in different amounts.) Estrogen brings about the development of both the external and internal sex organs and that of the secondary sex characteristics.

The progesterone produced by the corpus luteum prepares the lining of the uterus, the endometrium, for the fertilized egg; it induces secretions, and the soft mucous lining becomes thickened and spongy with an increased blood supply. If the egg is fertilized, the corpus luteum continues to produce progesterone for about four months, then the *placenta* [plah-sen′tah] takes over the job. If the egg is not fertilized, the lining built up by the progesterone from the corpus luteum is sloughed off and carried away in the menstrual flow.

Menstruation

We have discussed how the FSH affects the follicles of the ovaries and mentioned that if the egg is not fertilized the lining of the uterus that was built up to nourish the embryo is then shed through the process of menstruation. Menstruation begins at puberty or *menarche* [me-nar′ke], and it ends in the late forties or early fifties with the *menopause* [men′o-pawz].

The average *menstrual cycle* is twenty-eight days, but it is normal for it to vary from twenty-one to thirty-five or more days, and cases of six-month cycles, even one-year cycles, have been recorded. The menstrual cycle has three phases: the *proliferative* [pro-lif'-er-a-tiv] or preovulatory, the *secretory* [se-kre'to-re] or postovulatory, and the bleeding or *menses* [men'sez].

The first phase starts on the first day of menstruation and lasts for about two weeks. During this time the hypophysis secretes FSH, which stimulates the follicles and prepares one of them to ripen. At the same time the ovary is producing estrogen which causes the endometrium to become thicker. (At the end of a menstrual period this lining is about $\frac{1}{25}$ inch thick; this becomes about $\frac{4}{25}$ inch thick before the end of the cycle and the beginning of the next period of menstruation.) Ovulation, which occurs when the ovarian follicle ruptures, is the end of the first phase.

The second phase lasts about ten days and during this time the corpus luteum produces progesterone which takes over the task of stimulating the endometrium to secrete its special mucus and to increase its blood supply in readiness for the fertilized egg. If fertilization does not occur, there is, of course, no need for this preparation, and the third phase ensues. By the time the unfertilized egg reaches the uterus the corpus luteum has ceased its production of progesterone, and within a few days the uterus begins to shed the thickened lining and menstruation begins.

Menstruation may last from three to seven days, but, as with the cycle, it varies from individual to individual. The periods may be quite irregular for a year or so after the menarche. However, they become more regular both as to the number of days between periods and the number of days of the period as a girl gets older. Even then there may be minor variations of the pattern due to emotional stress or physical health. The menstrual flow—not a very accurate term as the amount totals no more than a few tablespoons—

consists of blood, broken-down pieces of tissue, mucus, and bacteria. The flow has the appearance of fresh blood, sometimes with small clots; it starts slowly, usually reaches its maximum on the second day, and tapers off toward the end of the period. As the discharge leaves the cervix there is no odor, but it becomes odorous after exposure to the air. It is normal that there may be some discomfort just before and during the first few days of the menstrual period—cramps in the abdomen, backache, or headache—proper posture and daily exercise help to correct this.

Disposable sanitary napkins or pads made of cellulose to absorb the flow are available commercially. It may be of interest to note that these were not commercially developed until after World War I. During the war cotton was in short supply and cellulose (wood and other plant fibers) pads were used for surgical dressings in France. The nurses in these French hospitals found these cellulose pads made excellent sanitary napkins. Previous to that time women folded a piece of cloth (frequently a square of birdseye, as was used then for diapers), washed the cloth, and used it again until it wore out. In more recent years tampons have been developed. A tampon is a small roll of soft surgical cotton with an attached cord. This is enclosed in a smooth container-applicator, which is inserted into the vagina so that the top of the tampon comes in contact with the cervix. The container is then removed, leaving the tampon in place with its cord remaining outside the body for easy removal.

Tampons generally cannot be used by younger girls, and, as opinions vary about the use of these, a physician should be consulted. In fact, it must be emphasized that any questions an individual may have regarding menstruation should be discussed with a physician. He is well qualified to assure one if there is nothing to worry about and to prescribe remedies if he believes they are necessary.

It is interesting to note that primitive women used essentially similar devices for controlling the menstrual flow. Clumps of soft moss were crushed, pressed against the vagina, and then burned secretly in the woods by the Maori women of New Zealand. In Central Africa women held clumps of soft vegetable fibers in place by a piece of goatskin and a twisted thong. In Indonesia balls of soft vegetable fibers were used as tampons. The most common method, however, was a piece of cloth as used in this country up to less than fifty years ago.

At the time of the menopause, or *climacteric* [kli'mak-ter'ik], the menstrual periods become irregular and of shorter duration with a scanty flow until finally they stop altogether. This is considered to be the end of a woman's reproductive life, although ovulation may continue for a few years and therefore pregnancy is possible after the menopause. Although there may be some discomfort associated with it, the menopause is as normal a process as is the menarche; it does not affect sex relations, and there is no reason for a woman to be upset by it.

Breasts

We have mentioned that the hormones play an important role in the development of secondary sex characteristics in both males and females. One of the most important of these in the female is the *breasts*, or *mammary* [mam'er-e] *glands*, which will be discussed now, although they do not directly have anything to do with reproduction.

In six-week human embryos there is a thickening called the milk ridge or milk line on each side of the body running between the limb buds (the beginning of the arms and legs). After the eighth week only that part of the milk ridge which will form the two breasts remains. These remain undeveloped in the male, although sometimes one or both may enlarge somewhat during puberty—generally this enlargement disappears of its own accord within two years.

The development of the female breasts starts about two years before the menarche. In a previous section devoted to the ovaries we learned that at puberty the hypophysis begins secreting three gonadotropic hormones, two of which were discussed in connection with the function of the ovaries. The third, the LTH or prolactin, is an essential component of the hormone combination that brings about the development of the breasts. Prolactin helps maintain the corpus luteum, which is responsible for the production of progesterone; and it also supplements the estrogen and progesterone in the mammary development. Estrogen stimulates the formation of fat and connective tissue. During pregnancy progesterone in conjunction with other hormones stimulates the formation of the milk-secreting cells, and prolactin starts the secretion of the milk.

The breasts are, in technical terms, superficial to the *pectoralis* [pek'to-ra'lis] *major*—a huge muscle in the chest—and generally extend from the second through the sixth rib and from the side of the sternum (breastbone) to the edge of the armpit. The left one is frequently slightly larger than the right. The breast is rounded or conical in shape and covered by soft skin; a little below its center is a *nipple,* surrounded by an area called the *areola* [ah-re'o-lah]. Both the nipple

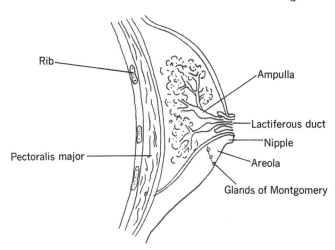

7.   *Duct system of the female breast. The figure shows the glands of Montgomery that occur in the areola which surrounds the nipple. Within the nipple are the lactiferous ducts extending from the ampullae, which store the milk.*

and the areola are darker than the rest of the breast, varying from pink to black depending upon the pigmentation of the individual. The size of the areola also varies with individuals—it may barely extend beyond the nipple or it may be quite large. During pregnancy the areola darkens; after pregnancy it may lighten somewhat, but it does not return to its original color. The surface of the areola appears rough because of the *glands of Montgomery* (named for William Fetherstone Montgomery, an Irish gynecologist—a physician specializing in the medical care of women—1797–1859), which are just beneath the skin and produce a lubricating substance to protect the nipple during suckling.

Furthermore, beneath the surface are smooth muscles which cause the nipple to become erect when stimulated, thus making suckling easier.

In addition to stimulating the formation of fat and connective tissue estrogen causes the duct system of the breast to develop. Within each nipple are 15 to 20 *lactiferous* [lak-tif′er-us] *ducts*, each of which expands near the nipple to form an ampulla, a reservoir for the storage of milk. The ampullae are extensions of the mammary ducts which reach toward the wall of the chest. During pregnancy tubules sprouting from these mammary ducts multiply to form the milk-secreting cells. By the time the baby is born the breasts are enlarged and ready to produce milk.

After delivery of the baby the prolactin, which has been kept in check by the estrogen and the placenta-produced progesterone, starts the secretion of milk; after a few days the suckling of the baby maintains the supply of milk. Just before the baby is born the breasts produce a thin, yellowish liquid called *colostrum* [ko-los′trum], which in addition to water contains nutrients—protein, fat, sugar, and salt—but not in the same proportions as in the milk which comes later. After delivery of the baby there is an increase in the amount of colostrum for a day or two, but by the third or fourth day only milk is being produced. This may amount to a quart or more a day. For both physiological and psychological reasons doctors encourage women to nurse their babies, especially for the first few months. However, if nursing is not possible, there are commercially prepared formulas available which are close approximations to human milk. As the continued production of milk depends on the suckling of the baby, whenever nursing is stopped the activity of the glands ceases and the breasts become smaller and less firm.

After the menopause the gland tissue gradually atrophies, but the duct system and connective tissue remain. The breasts become smaller and lose their rounded appearance until in elderly women they may be nothing more than skin pouches.

4. Coitus

Reproduction is one of the fundamental drives of life, and when an animal reaches sexual maturity it is ready to play its part in producing more of its kind. With the exception of some of the higher apes and man, most sexually-mature female animals have an *estrus* [es′trus] *cycle,* a regularly recurrent state of sexual excitability which is the only time that the female is interested in mating. This is not the same as the menstrual cycle of primates (the animal classification in which monkeys, apes, and humans are placed), but it does have a similar purpose— preparation of the uterus for the fertilized egg(s), ovulation, mating, and the beginning of embryonic growth.

The Estrus Cycle

Some animals have only one estrus cycle a year, apparently at the time which will result in the young being born in a favorable season. For example, a deer's cycle begins in October or November, and at one phase the doe will accept the buck's attention; she is in heat. Although the buck does not experience an estrus cycle, his body has been getting ready for the breeding season: during the spring and summer he has grown a new set of antlers, which he rubs and polishes; and, as the breeding season commences, he comes into rut (a state of sexual excitement)—his neck becomes enlarged and strong, he becomes belligerent and fights with other bucks. When the doe will accept his attention the two mate; and, as the *gestation* [jes-ta'shun] *period* is seven months, one or two fawns are born the following May or June.

Another example of the annual cycle is that of the fur seals of the Pribilof Islands in the Bering Sea. In early May the fat, sleek bulls arrive from the sea to await the females. Approximately a month later the cows, heavy with pup, put in an appearance and soon give birth to their young. About six days after the pups are born the females are in heat and ready to mate. Robert Hegner (1946:628) says:

> The home life of the Fur Seal would hardly be tolerated in human society. Polygamy is practiced, the bulls fighting fiercely with one another to establish a harem, which may contain up to 75 cows. The bachelors are forced to associate together until old enough and strong enough to displace one of the bulls. The cows occasionally enter the sea to feed, but the bulls neither eat nor drink for several months during the breeding season, but spend their time, both day and night, guarding their harem and ferociously battling with neighboring bulls in order to acquire more cows. Some animals apparently are never satisfied. Anyway, the strongest and most aggressive bulls leave offspring and in this way the vigor of the race is admirably maintained.

By the end of July when the mating season draws to a close the bulls are thin, worn-out, and scarred from fighting; in August they return to the sea to feed and rebuild their strength for the next year's mating activities. Meanwhile the cows continue to go to the sea to feed but return to their young at gradually lengthening intervals until November when the pups swim south with their mothers.

Domestic animals such as the cow and horse have more than one breeding season each year. If the female is not bred, she will have another estrus cycle within a certain number of days and be in heat again.

Although the human female does not have an estrus cycle and therefore does not experience a period of heat, some women have a greater desire for sexual intercourse at certain times during the menstrual cycle—perhaps, similar to but not as intense as the estrus cycle of animals. However, the human female's acceptance is not confined to a certain span of time; nor is the human male's interest restricted to a period of rut—both are attracted to each other and willing to engage in sexual relations at any time.

Mating among Human Beings

As we know, mating among human beings is referred to as coitus, or sexual intercourse or sexual relations, indicating that more is involved than in the instinctive mating of animals. While man's anatomy and physiology are similar to that of other mammals, the mating of a man and a woman involves the emotions, especially love, which make the act of intercourse more than an animal experience. Sexual intercourse is more than an instinctive act; it is a deeply personal relationship, the most intimate way of expressing the affection between a husband and wife, and therefore done in privacy. Religions have set up codes which look upon sexual relations outside of marriage as being immoral. Our discussion will be concerned with coitus within the married state.

The Male's Response

During lovemaking the male and female indulge in petting—known as *foreplay*—to stimulate the sexual urge. (Because of the intimate nature of sex relations cleanliness of the body and external genitalia is a necessity.) As both persons become prepared for coitus, their bodies may release secretions to lubricate the sex organs.

Under sexual excitement the spongy tissue of the penis becomes engorged with blood, causing it to become rigid and erect and to increase in length and diameter. In this condition it is possible for the male to insert the penis into the vagina of the female. Highly complex emotional factors associated with the sex drive, love for the other person, and body contact combine to bring about a surge of feeling which results in an *orgasm* [or′gazm]; at that moment muscular contractions force the semen out of the penis in spurts.

The Female's Response

The female also reacts to lovemaking, resulting in the clitoris becoming rigid and somewhat erect. Due to stimulation of this and other parts of the body such as the breasts and lips, she, too, can experience an orgasm—sort of a neural explosion, not accompanied by any release of fluid as in the male. Modern women usually expect and attain just as much enjoyment from their sex life as do men.

In most cases a woman's sexual feelings are not as easily aroused as a man's and for this reason a husband must learn how to stimulate his wife so she too can enjoy a gratifying sex life. Mutual love and respect of man and woman for each other within marriage make a satisfactory sex life possible. With experience the couple learns to adjust to each other and to work out a relationship which results in complete sexual satisfaction for both.

Conception

Physiologists now know that most pregnancies occur when sexual relations take place during the middle of the menstrual cycle (at the time of ovulation). However, this time of ovulation and subsequent pregnancy is not true for all women, for ovulation may occur on any day between the end of one menstrual period and the onset of the next. Curtis and Huffman (1950:133) wrote, "An *absolutely* 'safe period' does not exist. There is a *relatively* 'safe period' which lasts for approximately one week preceding menstruation; there is a slightly less safe period of a few days immediately following menstruation." At present there is no sure way of knowing when ovulation takes place. Physiologists believe the body temperature increases at the time of ovulation.

If a couple is desirous of having a child, they will not use any method of birth control; the sperm will ascend the female reproductive tract so that fertilization may take place. The 200,000,000 or more sperm, having been deposited at the upper end of the vagina, are near the opening of the cervix. Not only is the survival of the sperm dependent on their own quality but also on the secretions and reactions of the female genital tract. The sperm leave the alkaline environment of the male genital tract and meet their first hazard, an acid environment of the vagina. However, in less than 2 minutes some of the sperm are in the cervix, which at midcycle provides an alkaline environment. It is not entirely understood how the sperm get through the uterus and into the fallopian tubes within 30 minutes. Sperm are relatively immobile in the male body, but in the female body they become active and swim in tadpole fashion in the semen, probably assisted in their voyage to the uterine cavity by contractions of the uterus. To reach the fallopian tubes the sperm have to go faster against the outward motion of the cilia of the tubes; uterine action and secretions may help in getting the sperm into the tubes.

It is believed that a few thousand sperm succeed in reaching the correct tube near the ovulated egg. (It should be understood that a sperm may eventually unite with the egg even if no orgasm is experienced by the female.) The question arises as to how long sperm and egg are viable, that is, for how long do they have the capacity to unite? In the female reproductive tract sperm can remain alive for two to four days (even up to seven days, according to some authorities), but it is doubtful that the fertilizing power lasts more than from 48 to 72 hours. The egg probably cannot be fertilized after 24 hours from its release. Patten (1958:70) states "the best information at present available indicates that the human ovum does not retain its capacity to be fertilized much over a day after its discharge from the ovary."

The meeting of the sperm and the ovum appears to be simply by chance. The sperm swarm about the egg in the tube and probably several penetrate the egg cover with the aid of an *enzyme* [en′zim], *hyaluronidase* [hi′ah-lu-ron′ĭ-dās], in the semen. However, the head with its *chromosome* [kro′mo-sōm] load of only one sperm will reach the nucleus to fertilize the egg. When the sperm unites with the egg, the tail drops off, and a fertilization membrane that prevents the entrance of any other sperm is developed. The two cells (egg and sperm) become one cell, a *zygote* [zi'got]—from Greek, meaning "yoked (or joined) together"—and a new individual is created.

5. Human Embryology

As soon as the egg is fertilized a remarkable series of events begins to take place, following each other in precise order, until ultimately a fully-developed fetus is ready to be born. The study of this process is known as *embryology* [em'bre-ol'o-je], one of the very interesting branches of biology.

Embryonic Period

Cleavage Stage

The process of *cleavage* [klēv'ij] starts even as the fertilized egg, or zygote, is moving from the fallopian tube toward the uterus. The single, fertilized egg develops into a many-celled embryo by dividing to form two cells, then four, eight, sixteen, and so on. The cleavage is so rapid that there is no time for the growth of individual cells. Therefore, although the number of cells increases, there is little change in the size of the total cellular mass. A noncellular membrane, the *zona pellucida* [zo'nah pel-lu'sid-ah], surrounds and limits the size of this rounded cellular mass. The mass of cells, called a *morula* [mor'u-lah]—from Latin, meaning "mulberry"—reaches the uterus three to five days after fertilization.

Blastocyst Stage

The *blastocyst* [blas'to-sist] *stage* occurs after the

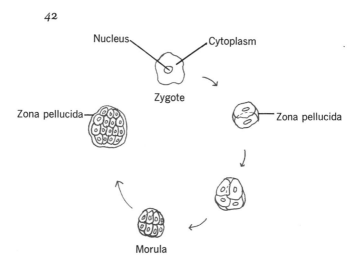

8. *Development of the fertilized egg during the cleavage stage. The zygote, or fertilized egg, with the nucleus in the center is shown at the top. Looking in a clockwise direction, it can be noted how, although limited somewhat in size by the zona pellucida, the zygote rapidly divides into two, four, etc. cells.*

morula enters the uterus. The interior of the morula becomes hollow as the mass of cells divides into two parts. One part, which will develop into the embryo, is a solid ball of cells (the inner cell mass). This ball is suspended inside and attached to the upper edge of the other part—the outer sphere of cells—which will become the outer membrane.

Inner Cell Mass This mass of cells divides simultaneously into two adjoining masses: 1] the *ectoderm* [ek′to-derm], outer skin, which will cover the outer surface of the body; and 2] the *endoderm* [en′do-derm], inner skin, which will, to some degree, line the inner surface.

The portion of the ectoderm nearest to the endoderm

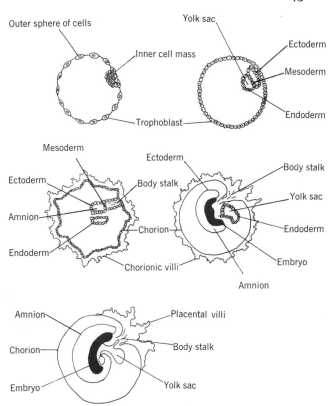

9.   *Development of the embryo during the blastocyst stage (drawings greatly enlarged). In the top left diagram the morula becomes hollow as the cells continue to divide. The cells of the outer membrane invade the zona pellucida to form the trophoblast. The top right indicates how the inner cell mass develops, while the middle left drawing continues the development with the amnion and chorion shown. The body stalk, which will become the umbilical cord, appears in the middle figures. The bottom diagram indicates the development of the placental villi.*

grows larger as the cells multiply and eventually forms the outer skin and nervous system. The rest of the ectoderm forms the wall of a fluid-filled cavity which expands to envelop the whole embryo. This inner surrounding membrane is the *amnion* [am'ne-on], and its fluid is the *amniotic* [am'ne-ot'ik] *fluid.*

In the region between the ectoderm and the endoderm some cells form a tissue, the *mesoderm* [mes'o-derm]. This is destined to form the body's connective tissue — including bone, muscles, blood and blood vessels.

Outer Membrane   While the inner cell mass is developing to form the embryo, the cells of the outer membrane begin to invade the zona pellucida. This action creates a one-cell thick *trophoblast* [trof'o-blast] — from two Greek words meaning "germ nourishment" — which takes the place of the zona pellucida.

As we learned in Chapter 3, the progesterone produced by the corpus luteum has prepared the endometrium for the fertilized egg; and about three to four days after it reaches the uterus, the blastocyst becomes attached to this lining. Six to seven days after fertilization, *implantation* [im'plan-ta'shun] takes place: the blastocyst penetrates and sinks into the endometrium, and the uterine tissues grow to cover the spot of penetration.

Nourishment of the Embryo/Fetus

In the chicken, the large yolk mass of the egg provides food for the development of the embryo; but the yolk mass of the human egg is too small to serve this purpose.

Placenta   As the blastocyst sinks into the lining of the uterus, the trophoblast, in contact with the uterus, develops into the *chorion* [ko're-on]. The chorion becomes covered with tiny, branching *villi* [vil'i], which fasten themselves into the blood-rich lining of the uterus.

As growth continues, the embryo, floating in the amniotic fluid, and the two surrounding membranes (the inner amnion and the outer chorion) push out into the cavity of the uterus. This causes the villi to disappear except where contact with the uterus is maintained. The portion of the chorion retaining the villi plus the part of the uterus wall to which they are attached becomes the placenta—the equivalent of a combination of lungs, kidneys, and food passage to the unborn child.

In the placenta thin partitions separate the blood of the embryo/fetus from that of the mother. These partitions, although not allowing for interchange of blood, do permit a rapid interchange of oxygen, carbon dioxide, food, and waste matter.

Umbilical Cord   As the inner cell mass is dividing into the ectoderm and the endoderm, a group of cells forms the *body stalk,* a tube from the yolk sac to the chorion. This body stalk lengthens to become the *umbilical* [um-bil'ĭ-kal] *cord,* which provides a connecting tube between the embryo/fetus and the placenta. The cord is not hollow but contains two arteries carrying deoxygenated blood and one vein carrying oxygenated blood.

Hormonal Activity of Placenta

The placenta not only provides nourishment for the unborn child, but it also produces hormones—estrogen, progesterone, and *chorionic gonadotropin* [ko're-on'ik gon'ah-do-tro'pin], all necessary for the continuation of the pregnancy.

Estrogen prevents the development of additional graafian follicles during pregnancy, thus ovulation does not occur. Progesterone helps maintain the lining of the uterus so the embryo finds attachment, develops, and does not abort. Both hormones help to prepare the breasts to produce milk after the baby is born.

During the first two months of pregnancy the chorionic gonadotropin keeps the corpus luteum actively producing both estrogen and progesterone. Later, less chorionic gonadotropin is produced, and consequently the corpus luteum is less active. By that time the placenta is producing enough estrogen and progesterone to maintain the uterine lining.

Growth During the Embryonic Period

Even in the third week after conception the beginnings of many organs are present. The fastest growing area is that which will become the head and the brain. This more rapid development of the head compared to other parts of the body continues until after birth.

The Fourth Week   By this time all the internal organs (heart, liver, brain, etc.) are really taking form. The heart is beating, although it will be many weeks before it can be heard.

The Fifth Week   There is a distinct archlike bend to the embryo's body. The backbone starts to develop; the limb buds (the beginnings of the arms and legs) have appeared.

The Sixth Week   The embryo is about ½ inch long, with a tail and a potbelly, because the internal organs are growing so fast. Arms and legs with tiny webbed fingers and toes have developed from the limb buds.

The Seventh Week   The face takes on a more definite shape; the eyelids and ears are forming. The internal organs begin to take permanent positions.

Fetal Period

By the end of eight weeks the basic plan of the external features and internal systems is present. Since it is now possible to recognize the developing organism as a human being, it is referred to as a fetus. This is the period of fast growth in size.

The Ninth to Thirteenth Week   The fingers and toes lose their webs, the tail has disappeared, and the body grows longer. The fetus is about 2½ inches long and weighs about ½ ounce.

The Fourteenth to Seventeenth Week   The fingers and toes are well formed, and the nails begin to appear. The head is becoming more erect, although the body is still archlike. A little hair is growing on the scalp, and the external sex organs have developed. By the end of this period the fetus is 4 to 5 inches long and weighs about 4 ounces.

The Eighteenth to Fortieth Week   At about twenty weeks the fetus is approximately 8 inches long and weighs about 10½ ounces. As a full-term baby will weigh at least 5½ pounds and be about 20 inches long, these months are ones of very rapid growth. From the twenty-second week on the entire body is covered with soft downy hair which disappears before birth. During the last eight weeks the body fat is formed, and the skin becomes less red and wrinkled. At birth the more natural-color skin will still be covered with a soft, creamy secretion, called *vernix caseosa* [ver'niks ka'se-o'sah]—from Latin, meaning "cheesy varnish." This secretion has protected the skin of the unborn child for the forty weeks.

6. Pregnancy

The development of the embryo/fetus was discussed in the previous chapter; we shall now consider the changes and adaptations that occur in the mother.

Tests for Pregnancy

One indication of pregnancy is, of course, the cessation of the menstrual periods; but there are tests for pregnancy, some of which are mainly of historical interest at the present time, as they have been replaced by simpler tests. One of these tests of historical interest, developed in 1933, involves the use of a male grass frog. A small amount of a woman's first urine of the morning is injected into the frog. If the urine contains gonadotropic hormones from the placenta, the grass frog will emit sperm into its own urinary bladder. Every 30 minutes for 3 hours a small amount of urine is withdrawn from the frog and examined with a microscope. If sperm are found in the urine, the woman is probably pregnant.

In another test concentrated urine from the woman is injected into the ear of a female rabbit on two successive days. After 24 hours the rabbit is anesthetized and its ovaries are examined; if bleeding or ruptured follicles are noted, the woman is considered to be pregnant.

Two Germans developed one of the most accurate tests for pregnancy; the Aschheim-Zondek test is almost infallible. In this test concentrated urine from the woman is injected into four immature, female mice on three consecutive days. The mice are then killed and their ovaries examined. If the ovaries of at least one animal contain *hemorrhagic* [hem'o-raj'ik] *follicles* or if corpus luteum is present, the test indicates pregnancy.

More recently tests have been developed which do not require the use of animals. The most widely used one is based on the fact that a pregnant woman will produce a large amount of chorionic gonadotropin, the pregnancy hormone. A sample of the woman's urine, mixed with specially prepared chemicals, will cause the formation of a precipitate which will be present only if the patient is pregnant. The test is simple, quick, and accurate in 95 per cent to 98 per cent of the cases.

Another test involves taking pills for three days. The pills contain large amounts of estrogen and progesterone. If the patient does not have a normal menstrual period within a week after this, there is a 90 per cent chance that she is pregnant.

Ectopic Pregnancy

Occasionally a pregnancy will occur outside of the uterus; this is called an *ectopic* [ek-top'ik] —meaning out of normal place— *pregnancy*. The most common type is a tubal pregnancy—the fertilized egg becomes implanted in the fallopian tube and grows there. Eventually the tube will rupture. On rare occasions the egg may become implanted on the ovary—an ovarian pregnancy. An abdominal pregnancy usually occurs when a tubal pregnancy breaks through the tube wall and is implanted on the inner wall of the abdomen, on the outer wall of the uterus, on the intestines, or on the broad ligament. Any ectopic pregnancy requires medical attention and must be terminated by surgery.

Abortion

Sometimes during pregnancy the embryo or fetus may be expelled from the uterus before it is time for it to be born; this is a *spontaneous abortion* [spon-ta'ne-us ah-bor'shun], often referred to as a *miscarriage*. Sometimes because the woman's health or even life is endangered it is necessary to remove the embryo or fetus by surgery; this is termed a *therapeutic* [ther'ah-pu'tik] *abortion*. Abortions performed on women to rid them of an unwanted embryo or fetus are called *criminal abortions;* at the present time in the United States they are criminal offenses and punishable by law.

Normal Pregnancy

Since most pregnancies are normal we shall consider the usual aspects of this process. The uterus of a woman who has never been pregnant has a capacity of less than a teaspoon and weighs about 2 ounces. As the embryo/fetus grows larger, the muscles of the uterine wall stretch so the uterus increases about 20 times in size. By the end of the gestation period the upper part of the uterus extends to the bottom of the breastbone and the organ weighs between 2 and 3 pounds and will hold from 5 to 7 quarts of liquid. Externally, this causes a pronounced expansion of the woman's abdominal region and a consequent shift in balance; to compensate for this shift the woman becomes somewhat swaybacked. Internally, the stomach, liver, and intestines adapt to the enlargement of the uterus.

Usually the fertilized egg is implanted on the front or back of the broader, upper part of the uterus. Sometimes implantation is on either sidewall but rarely is it near the cervix.

The mother's diet has an effect on the development of the unborn child whose growth is dependent on the food secured from the mother. As the bones form, there is an increased demand for calcium; if this demand is not met by sufficient calcium in the mother's diet, the mother's body will draw on her own bones to supply the deficiency. As pregnancy progresses the cardiac output of the mother increases to supply more blood, with its food and oxygen, to the placenta.

Medical science has no place for such superstitions as the idea that evil thoughts on the part of the mother can affect the mind of the growing fetus; that pinching or bruising the mother's skin will cause a birthmark at exactly the same spot on the baby; that hocus-pocus or hexing can deform the child; or that the mother's wishful thinking can control the sex of the baby.

In discussing the ovaries in the chapter on the female reproductive system we noted how the corpus luteum and the placenta produce progesterone to prepare and maintain the endometrium so the fertilized egg can develop properly. In fact, pregnancy seems to be chemically controlled by hormones, but there is still much to be learned about them and their functions.

Normally the embryo/fetus assumes a head downward position in the uterus with arms and legs folded and eyelids closed. In the fifth month of pregnancy the fetal heartbeat at the rate of about 140 per minute can be heard with a *stethoscope* [steth′o-skōp], and the mother will be able to feel faint, fluttering movements, known as *quickening*. By the sixth month these movements will become thumps as the fetus kicks and changes position frequently—sometimes its head may be up, sometimes down—but later it will settle in one position until birth.

Obstetrics [ob-stet′riks] is the branch of medicine dealing with birth, and a physician specializing in this field is called an *obstetrician* [ob′stĕ-trish′un]. Although pregnancy is a normal physiological process and generally no difficulties are encountered, a woman must not delay in seeing a doctor either in his office or at a clinic. A well-trained physician will want to know about the patient's health (past and present) as well as that of other members of the family. A complete physical examination will be made, probably on the first visit, and additional examinations will be made at regular intervals during and after pregnancy. If necessary, the doctor will prescribe a diet to aid in the development of a normal, healthy baby. Present-day research indicates that many birth defects can be prevented by proper prenatal care. In addition, the physical examinations alert the physician to any problems which may arise during or immediately after delivery.

7. Birth

Labor

Approximately 280 days after the beginning of the last menstrual period contractions of the uterine musculature begin – the onset of *labor*. No completely satisfactory explanation has been given for the beginning of labor. It is probably a combination of neural and hormonal processes and physical stretch. Labor may last, on the average, from 12 to 18 hours and is divided into three stages.

Stage of Dilation

This is the longest stage of labor when the cervix, which has softened and relaxed during pregnancy, dilates to allow the fetus to pass from the uterus into the vagina. The rhythmic contractions of the uterus push the fetus into the lower end of the uterus; this pressure usually causes the *amniotic sac* (also, referred to as the *bag of waters*) to rupture, sending a quart or more of fluid through the vagina.

The contractions – *labor pains* – become more frequent and intense, and gradually, as the fetal head presses against it, the cervix opens until it is fully dilated to a diameter of about 4 inches.

Stage of Descent

During this stage, which is much shorter than the first, the abdominal muscles also begin to contract.

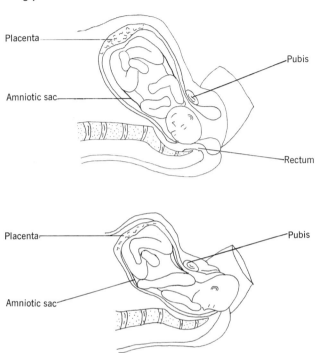

10. *Fetal positions during labor. The top drawing shows the fetus during the stage of dilation. The fetus exerts a pressure mainly forward, and the rectum is kept open. The bottom drawing shows the fetus during the stage of descent. As the fetus is pushed into the vagina and the head emerges, the pressure is against the rectum, which is now closed.*

The mother feels like bearing down and pushing with each contraction and thus helps the birth process. There is plenty of room for the passage of the fetus because during the last weeks of pregnancy the pelvic joints have become more pliable, and during labor the urethra is pressed against the pubic bone and the rectum against the backbone. (The physician may give the mother a drug to ease any pain, and an anesthetic may be administered in the final minutes before the baby is born.)

The fetus is pushed into the vagina; the head reaches the opening and emerges. The doctor provides what guidance and turning may be necessary to bring first the head and then the body through the dilated vaginal opening. After the baby is born the physician clamps the umbilical cord and cuts it, leaving a short stump which will dry up and fall off in a few days—the place of attachment is marked by the *navel* [na′vel].

Placental Stage

The third stage, usually occurring within 20 minutes of the birth of the child, is the discharge of the *afterbirth*—the placenta, the umbilical cord, the amniotic sac, and other membranes. The uterine contractions continue after delivery and bring about the separation of the placenta from the uterine wall. The afterbirth is expelled and examined by the physician to make sure that it has separated properly.

Breech Birth

Generally the child is born with the head, which is the largest part of his body, first. However, sometimes the baby is born buttocks first, a *breech birth*. In this case the doctor must manipulate the body so that the fetus does not suffocate as the head comes through the cervix. The umbilical cord is pressed tightly between the head and the cervix with the result that the supply of circulating blood is cut off. Consequently the physician must help to get the head through the cervix as quickly as possible.

Caesarean Section

Occasionally the mother's pelvis is too small for the baby to be born in the usual way; in this case a *caesarean* [se-za're-an] *section* is performed by a surgeon. An incision is made through the abdominal wall and into the uterus, and the baby and afterbirth are lifted out through this opening.

"Legend has it that Julius Caesar was born by such surgery, but in those days the operation was performed only on women who died in labor, and by Caesar's own account, his mother was alive when he was 48 years old. Other popular explanations: if a Roman woman died pregnant, the operation was required by the emperor's law—*Lex Caesarea*—thus a caesarian section. Or the name may be derived from the Latin verb *caedere,* to cut" (*Time,* June 7, 1963, 52).

Premature Babies

Some babies are born before term, earlier than the approximately 280 days. These *premature babies* must be put in an incubator and given special attention for several weeks. If properly cared for, they will grow and develop as normally as a full-term baby.

Involution

After the expulsion of the afterbirth the uterus begins to shrink. Within a week it has lost about 50 per cent of its weight, and at the end of six weeks it will have decreased from the weight of 2 pounds to about 2 ounces—nearly its prepregnancy size. During this process, *lochia* [lo'ke-ah], a combination of blood, mucus, and bits of the lining of the uterus will be discharged through the vagina for a few weeks. This period of gradual reduction in the size of the uterus is known as *involution* [in′vo-lu′shun].

Return of Menstruation

If a woman is not breast-feeding her baby, menstruation will begin again four to six weeks after delivery. If the baby is being breast-fed, the mother may not menstruate for about three months, and sometimes not then. However, even if she is not menstruating, the ovaries begin to function again, ovulation takes place, and another pregnancy can be started.

The Baby's Adjustments

At birth the average baby weighs about 7 pounds and is approximately 20 inches long. The heart beats at a rate of about 140 per minute, and the respiration rate varies from 30 to 35 per minute. The baby has left the uterine environment where it was completely dependent on its mother and now has to adjust to a series of rather spectacular physiological changes.

Lungs

The lungs have to take over the exchange of gases. Prior to birth the lungs were not inflated, but with the first gasp air rushes in, the exchange of carbon dioxide for oxygen begins, and the small lungs begin expanding; it may be several days before they are fully inflated. The first breath may be due to an accumulation of carbon dioxide in the blood or to the cooler air of the atmosphere stimulating the skin; it may be a continuation of fetal respiratory movements. Oxygen may be forced into the lungs with a tube in cases of delayed breathing.

Circulatory System

One of the most profound changes involves the circulatory system. The heart beats and the blood circulates in the fetus, but there is no convincing evidence as yet for oxygen-carbon dioxide exchange in the lungs. Blood with its carbon dioxide load is pumped through the paired umbilical arteries to the placenta, there to lose the carbon dioxide and take on a supply of oxygen. This blood then returns to the fetal body through the umbilical vein. Since the lungs are nonfunctioning, circulation in the heart is modified. Between the right and left *atria* [a'tre-ah], or *auricles* [aw're-k'lz], there is an opening, the *foramen ovale* [fo-ra'men o-va'le] — meaning egg-shaped opening — by which blood entering the fetal heart is diverted into the left atrium rather than being sent through the right *ventricle* [ven'trĭ-k'l] and pulmonary artery to the nonfunctioning lungs. Also, any blood that might get into the pulmonary artery is shunted through a connecting tube, the *ductus arteriosus* [duk'tus ar-te're-os'ūs], into the great *aorta* [a-or'tah]. Thus, fetal deoxygenated blood (incorrectly called blue blood) is by-passed into the general circulation and from there to the placenta for purification.

At birth the foramen ovale between the atria closes by means of flaps, causing the blood to go from the right side of the heart to the lungs, thence back to the left side of the heart and into the general circulation. The ductus arteriosus also closes, and thus normal pulmonary circulation involving the lungs is started.

Occasionally the foramen ovale does not close as it

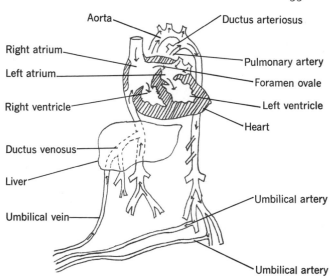

11.   *Circulatory system of the fetus. After birth one of the most profound changes takes place in this system. Note the position of the foramen ovale between the atria. Both the foramen ovale and the ductus arteriosus close at birth.*

should, thus permitting the deoxygenated blood of the right atrium to mix with the oxygenated blood of the left atrium. The result is that the blood that passes into the general circulation is deficient in oxygen, causing the infant's skin to be blue—a blue baby. Modern surgical techniques make it possible to enter the heart and repair the foramen ovale, thus bringing about normal heart function and skin color. An unclosed ductus arteriosus can also be corrected.

Digestive System

Until birth the fetus never digested a drop of milk or a spoonful of food, as the mother did this for it. With the first mouthful of milk the digestive system begins to function and actively secrete enzymes which will change the milk into nutrients usable by the body cells.

The kidneys now eliminate the wastes that were formerly carried to the placenta. Not only must the body get rid of wastes produced by living cells, but it must also dispose of unusable parts of food.

Nervous System

The nervous system is not even complete at birth, but the newborn infant soon reacts to certain stimuli. Later, as the baby becomes acquainted with his environment, he is able to see, hear, and feel.

Breast Feeding

At the end of the chapter on the female reproductive system we noted how the hormonal activity of a pregnant woman increases and prepares the breasts to produce milk. After the baby is born and the afterbirth with its progesterone-producing placenta has been expelled the estrogen level falls and the prolactin can start the secretion of milk.

Mothers may nurse their babies for a few days, weeks, or months to as long as a year. With the cessation of the suckling stimulus the production of milk decreases, ovarian activity builds up the estrogen level, the production of prolactin is inhibited, and the breasts cease to produce milk. When a child is taken from the breast-milk diet, he is said to be *weaned*.

During the first week or two of his life the infant will probably lose several ounces in weight. Following this period the baby usually begins to grow rapidly; by the time he is six months old he will weigh twice as much as at birth.

8. Multiple Birth, Sex Determination, and Rh Factor

As questions are frequently asked concerning the birth of more than one baby at a time, why a baby is a boy or a girl, and what is the importance of the Rh factor, brief discussions of each follow.

Multiple Birth

One of the more fascinating aspects of birth is the arrival of *twins*, *triplets* [trip′lets], *quadruplets* [kwod′ru-plets], or *quintuplets* [kwin′tu-plets]. *Sextuplets* [seks′tu-plets], *septuplets* [sep′tu-plets], and *octuplets* [ok′tu-plets] have been born, but all have either been born dead or have died shortly after birth. The figures given for the frequency of multiple birth do not take into account the use of any medication to increase fertility.

Twins

About one out of every 86 pregnancies terminates in the birth of twins; approximately one third of these are identical twins.

Fraternal Twins When, during one menstrual cycle, two eggs are ovulated and fertilized by two separate sperm cells, fraternal twins will develop. Each embryo/fetus has its own placenta (although these

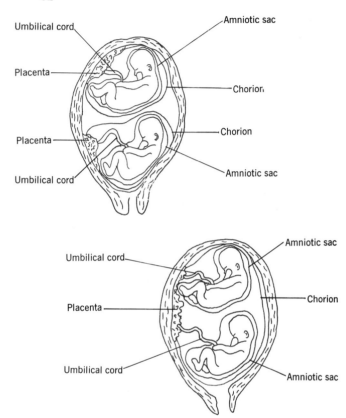

12.   *Uterine position of twins. The top drawing
shows fraternal twins with separate placentas,
chorions, and amniotic sacs. The bottom drawing shows identical twins with separate amniotic sacs but with only one chorion and one placenta.*

may be fused), chorionic membrane, and amniotic
sac. The babies may be of the same sex or of different
sexes, and they are no more alike than any *siblings*
[sib′linz], children born of the same parents.

Identical Twins The union of one egg and one sperm cell results in identical twins. Sometime in its very early development the fertilized egg splits in half—biologists are not sure whether this division takes place in the zygote, cleavage, or blastocyst stage. When this happens, each embryo/fetus has its own umbilical cord and, usually, amniotic sac; but they share the same placenta and chorionic membrane. Identical twins look exactly alike and are always of the same sex.

Siamese Twins One of the more unfortunate aspects of multiple birth is the arrival of *Siamese twins*—infants that are joined together. This may be due to an incomplete division of the inner cell mass with the result that some portion is shared by both embryos.

Such cases of incomplete twinning usually abort or die shortly after birth. When the joining does not involve vital organs or extensive tissue, surgical separation is possible. However, it is such a long complicated procedure that the babies generally do not survive.

The term Siamese twins is derived from a set of twins, Chang and Eng, born in Siam in 1811 to Chinese parents. Chang and Eng, joined at the waist by a band of cartilage, were for years with P. T. Barnum's circus. They married sisters and, according to *Collier's Encyclopedia*, fathered a total of nineteen children, all normal. After retirement from the circus Chang and Eng settled on a farm in North Carolina and died in 1874 within three hours of each other.

Triplets

The incidence of triplets is one in every 7396 births (86 times 86). Triplets may develop from one, two, or three eggs. If one egg splits to form three embryos, the result would be identical triplets. If two eggs are involved, two of the babies would be identical and one would be fraternal. Of course, fraternal triplets would be born from three eggs.

Quadruplets

The birthrate of quadruplets is one in 636,056 (86 times 86 times 86). Quadruplets could develop from one, two, three, or four eggs. One egg could divide into four cell masses. Two eggs could each split into two embryos; or one egg could divide into three, while the fourth baby developed from a second egg. One of three eggs could split to form two embryos while the other two eggs each developed separate embryos. The babies from the same egg would be identical; the others, fraternal.

Quintuplets

While the birth of quadruplets is a rare enough phenomenon to rate press releases throughout the world, the birth of quintuplets is an even more extraordinary event (rate of about one set every 54,000,000 births). The birth of more than triplets is important not only from the human-interest angle but from a biological standpoint, as it provides an opportunity for scientific study.

Almost any number of egg combinations could result in the birth of quintuplets, and the babies could be identical or fraternal—or both.

The most famous set of quintuplets, the Dionne girls, was born in 1934 in Canada. As they were delivered by a country doctor and were the first quintuplets to survive childhood, both the doctor and the girls received a great deal of publicity.

General Information

Plural births occur most often in the 35 to 39 year age group. They are least common below the age of 20 and above the age of 45.

Generally, one twin is stronger and weighs more at birth than the other, perhaps because the former was more favorably situated in the uterus.

As multiple births seem to run in families, apparently heredity has something to do with the phenomena.

Sex Determination

Heredity, the transmission of characteristics to an individual by his parents, is too complicated to be discussed in this book. Our knowledge of the field is continually increasing through scientific study. Therefore, we will consider only the factor of sex determination. As with multiple birth, heredity may play some part in the determination of sex, because only boys (or girls) may be born in several generations of a family.

The nucleus of each egg and sperm cell contains chromosomes, microscopically small bodies which carry the inherited traits of any individual. These chromosomes include ones which will determine the sex of the baby.

Each egg cell carries one X chromosome, and half the sperm cells have one X chromosome while the other half have one Y chromosome. If a sperm cell with an X chromosome unites with the egg cell, the result would be XX, a female. If a sperm cell with a Y chromosome unites with the egg cell, the result would be an XY combination, a male. Thus, the sperm determines the sex of the baby.

Rh Factor

Rh is the name for an inherited factor in the red blood cells of humans and higher animals. The symbol stands for Rhesus, as it was first detected in Rhesus monkeys, which are frequently used in laboratory research.

About 85 per cent of the Caucasian race (the percentage is higher for other races) has this Rh factor; these people are Rh positive. The 15 per cent who do not have this factor are Rh negative.

Much of the worry about the Rh factor is needless. If both the mother and the father are Rh positive or Rh negative, the child will experience no difficulties because of the Rh factor. There is only a slight possibility of trouble when the mother is Rh positive and the father is Rh negative.

Problems may occur with an Rh negative mother and an Rh positive father. However, even then there is no danger if the child inherits the Rh negative blood of the mother. Almost 50 per cent of the children born of such marriages will be Rh negative.

The only chance for danger is if the child inherits the father's Rh positive blood. In spite of the barrier afforded by the partitions of the placenta, a few cells of the positive blood get into the mother's bloodstream. When this happens, the system of the negative Rh mother starts producing antibodies against the positive Rh blood. These antibodies get into the child's bloodstream and tend to destroy his red blood cells. Generally, there is little trouble with the first child, as the mother's blood apparently does not develop enough antibodies to cause serious difficulty. However, enough antibodies may be developed to cause problems with subsequent children—lack of red blood cells may cause anemia or jaundice. Sometimes the destruction of the red blood cells occurs at a more rapid rate, and the child may be born dead.

Ever since the Rh factor was detected in the 1940's alert physicians check all pregnant women for the presence of this factor. If a woman's blood—usually checked on her first visit to the doctor—is Rh negative, her husband's is also checked. If his is Rh positive, the physician will check the mother's blood throughout the pregnancy to determine how much strength of antibodies (and how fast) her system is building up. If there are enough antibodies to cause trouble, preparations can be made to replace the baby's Rh positive blood at birth with a complete transfusion of Rh negative blood. In recent years a technique has been worked out whereby this transfusion can be given to the fetus while it is still in the uterus.

9. Venereal Disease

As other systems of the body may be affected by disease, so may the reproductive system. A discussion of such diseases has no place herein except for *venereal* [ve-ne′re-al] *diseases*, often called VD. Because of the increase in the incidence of venereal diseases in the United States, people must be made aware of the dangers of the two most common ones, *syphilis* [sif′ĭ-lis] and *gonorrhea* [gon′o-re′ah].

In 1954 it could be said that the number of cases of venereal disease had decreased in the previous two decades; but less than ten years later statistics showed such a marked increase that the *New York Times* noted "Epidemics of V.D. Plague 30 Cities; Federal Health Aides Note Sharp Rise Among Youth" (Dec. 13, 1964, Sec. 1, p. 73).

Syphilis

History

William F. Schwartz has found that the history of syphilis "dates back many centuries, perhaps to mankind's very beginnings. Plagues of syphilis have been responsible for millions of the world's crippled, blind, insane and dead. Throughout history, the spirochete has infected young, old, rich, and poor, showing no more respect for princes than for beggars" (*History of V.D.*, p. 1).

The term syphilis was used first in a poem written in 1530 by an Italian doctor to describe the sufferings of an afflicted shepherd called Syphilus.

Four hundred years ago people were asking where the disease came from and many answers were given —the conjunction of the planets Jupiter and Saturn in 1484, a curse from God, cannibalism, and others—all superstitious. So little was known about venereal diseases that some people believed syphilis and gonorrhea were two stages of the same disease. In 1767 one of England's famous physicians, Sir John Hunter, set out to prove that this was true and innoculated himself with pus from a gonorrhea patient. When the reputable doctor developed symptoms of both diseases, his theory seemed to be correct. (However, he had made an error in his experiment—his patient had syphilis as well as gonorrhea.)

In 1838 Philippe Ricord, a Baltimore physician working in France, proved after seven years of experiments that syphilis does not become gonorrhea and that they are two different diseases. "Then in 1879, Albert Neisser confirmed Ricord's experiments by proving that gonorrhea was caused by the coffee bean-shaped gonococcus, a bacterium; and in 1905, the German scientists, Drs. Fritz Schaudinn and Eric Hoffman saw and identified for the first time the germ which causes syphilis, a tiny, pale spirochete they called *Treponema pallidum*" (*History of V.D.*, p. 13).

Description of Organism

Treponema [trep'o-ne'mah] is a corkscrew-shaped organism, a *spirochete* [spi'ro-kēt]. As it is colorless and transparent and cannot be stained in its live state, it is almost impossible to see with a regular compound microscope. However, the organism can be seen with a top-lighted dark-field microscope, or it can be killed and stained for viewing with an ordinary microscope.

The organism lives in the blood and tissues of infected persons, and, if not treated, it will spread throughout the body.

Development of the Disease

In rare instances syphilis can be contracted by kissing an infected individual who has an open *chancre* [shang'ker], or sore, in his mouth. However, the disease is most frequently spread by direct contact during sexual intercourse—from the penis of the male to either the vulva or the vagina (or both) of the female or vice versa. After penetrating the moist surface of the penis, vagina, or vulva, the spirochete enters the bloodstream; and, if treatment is neglected, four stages will ensue.

First Stage The first sign of syphilis is usually a chancre appearing at the spot where the spirochetes entered the body. A chancre is a painless, ulcerlike *lesion* [le'zhun] with a raised rim. The inside of the chancre is smooth and shiny, and swarming with spirochetes. Chancres are usually located on the genital organs and appear from ten to thirty days (although it may take as long as ninety days) after intercourse. In the male, a chancre may be located on the penis or scrotum; in the female, it may be on the external genitalia, usually the labia majora, but it may also be in the vagina.

Sometimes there may be no chancre or the lesion may not be noticed because it is so small or because it is hidden deep inside a woman's sex organs. Also, because there is no discomfort, pain, or discharge, a chancre can be easily overlooked and thus, unknowingly, syphilis can be transmitted to a sexual partner in this very infectious primary stage. Within a few weeks the chancre will heal, even without treatment; an individual may think he is cured, but this is not true.

Second Stage   From three to six weeks later the second stage ensues after the organisms have entered the bloodstream and traveled to all parts of the body. Infectious lesions or sores may appear in the mouth (in this case, syphilis may be transmitted by kissing), and there may be a generalized rash over parts or all of the body. This may be so mild that it is mistaken for merely a heat rash, especially as there is no pain or discomfort even in this stage and the symptoms will disappear in time without treatment.

During this secondary stage, which may last for years, the spirochetes are being carried by the bloodstream into the deeper tissues of the internal organs, into the joints, eyes, arteries, brain, and spinal cord—anywhere in the body.

Third Stage   After the symptoms of the second stage disappear there is an apparent latent stage which may last from a few months to as long as twenty-five years. During this time the spirochetes continue their destruction of the body, attacking the heart, brain, and spinal cord.

Fourth Stage   The symptoms of this final stage of syphilis are many and varied but include circulatory diseases, crippling, blindness, and mental illness.

Even in the later stages of syphilis the disease can be cured, but previous damage to the body cannot be repaired.

Congenital Syphilis

Active syphilis cannot be inherited, but the spirochete from a syphilitic pregnant woman can be transmitted to the fetus through the placenta, and in that instance the baby will be born with *congenital* [kon-jen'ĭ-tal] *syphilis*. If the expectant mother receives treatment during pregnancy, the child will probably be normal. But if treatment is not received the fetus may abort or be born dead. If born alive, the child may have bodily defects or brain damage.

Diagnosis and Treatment

There are several tests for the detection of syphilis. The first blood test was developed in 1907 by August von Wasserman, a German bacteriologist. (Within the past thirty years most states have passed laws requiring applicants for marriage licenses and pregnant women to have blood tests.)

For several hundred years various cures for syphilis have been tried; often the cure turned out to be worse than the disease itself. In 1928 Dr. Alexander Fleming discovered penicillin, and thus began the age of antibiotics. In 1943 Dr. John Mahoney and his staff, at the U. S. Public Health Service Hospital on Staten Island, demonstrated that penicillin would cure syphilis; since that time other antibiotics have become available.

Gonorrhea

Gonorrhea, which has been a plague to mankind even longer than syphilis, is caused by a pus-forming bacterium, the *gonococcus* [gon'o-kok'us]. As with syphilis, the infection is acquired by sexual intercourse or close body contact.

Development of the Disease

The incubation period of gonorrhea is three to five days after infection. As the gonococci attack the mucous membrane lining of the penis, the first symptom a male may notice will be a painful, burning sensation when he urinates. The next symptom will be a visible one—a discharge of pus from the penis. Generally, the pain is severe enough to make an infected person seek medical advice.

The gonococci attack the mucous membrane of the vulva and vagina in the female, causing pus to form. Another site of infection may be the urethra, as it also opens directly into the vestibule of the vulva. Although there will be a discharge of pus from the vagina and there may be more frequent urination, generally the female does not have any noticeable symptoms or pain. If the disease is untreated, the infection may spread to the uterus and fallopian tubes.

Both men and women may become sterile as a result of gonorrhea. Occasionally, the disease will invade the bloodstream and carry the infection to various parts of the body, resulting in circulatory and crippling impairments, blindness, and even death.

During passage through the birth canal the eyes of newborn may become infected with *gonorrheal ophthalmia* [of-thal'me-ah], if the mother has gonorrhea. Many years ago this was a very common cause of blindness. In more recent years medication is applied to the baby's eyes shortly after birth, and this cause of blindness has virtually been eliminated.

Diagnosis and Treatment

As there is no practical blood test for gonorrhea, an examination of the discharge must be made under a microscope. Even this test is not foolproof as the gonococci may not be present in the specimen—repeated tests may be necessary.

Gonorrhea is treated with penicillin or one of the

other antibiotics, as is syphilis. Most early cases of the disease can be cured if treatment is begun *promptly*.

Precautionary Guidelines

It must be remembered that, although they are different diseases, both syphilis and gonorrhea

1. are contracted from infected persons;
2. are spread through sexual contact;
3. can be contracted any number of times during a lifetime;
4. are not self-limited (that is, having a definite course in a limited period) as measles or a cold, but will only get worse;
5. can cause serious physical and mental afflictions;
6. can be cured if treated immediately.

There is no known vaccine to protect us against any type of venereal disease. A person who has had one of the venereal diseases does not develop an immunity to that one or to any other venereal disease. In fact, as Sir John Hunter demonstrated two hundred years ago, it is quite possible to have both syphilis and gonorrhea at the same time.

Control of Venereal Disease

Every state has laws which require physicians to report all cases of venereal disease to health authorities; yet it is a well-known fact that the majority of diagnosed and treated cases are not reported. In addition, there are untold numbers of cases which have never been detected.

Even from the limited amount of evidence available it is obvious that venereal disease is found in all parts of the country, all races, all income classes, all age groups, and that the incidence among teenagers and young adults is increasing at an alarming rate.

The *History of V.D.* tells us:

> It is known now that, in 1962, regardless of the number reported, more than 100,000 persons were infected [with syphilis]. More than a million were infected with gonorrhea.
>
> One way or another, syphilis affects everyone . . . Those who do not suffer the effects of the disease must pay taxes to take care of many of those who do. For example, almost $50,000,000 a year is spent to maintain the syphilitic insane in tax-supported mental institutions.
>
> An additional $6,000,000 is spent by the government every year to help maintain the syphilitic blind. It is difficult to estimate how much more money is lost yearly due to the fact that most of the syphilitic insane and blind are not able to hold jobs and therefore do not pay taxes (p. 19).

In 1961, to combat the rising rate of infectious venereal disease, a Task Force was appointed to review the problem and make recommendations. The Task Force was particularly disturbed by four items,

1. Evidence of a chain reaction in the spread of syphilis infection, especially among teenagers;
2. Evidence that the unreported number of cases occurring far outnumber the reported cases;
3. Evidence that effective techniques of control and therapy to stop the spread of syphilis are available but are not applied widely enough;
4. Evidence that unless a vigorous, stepped-up campaign is inaugurated, the increased spread of syphilis may be accelerated.

The Task Force believed that the elimination of syphilis as a public health hazard requires an intensive and aggressive program based on two general areas of activity.

1. Control. Private physicians must report *all* the cases of syphilis they treat. In addition, all persons with whom the infected person may have had sexual contact must be found and treated (contact tracing).

2. Education. The public, as well as doctors, nurses, teachers, social workers, and ministers, must become informed of the seriousness and importance of a national campaign to eradicate venereal disease.

If these two suggestions were applied, the spread of syphilis (and gonorrhea), now of epidemic proportions, could be minimized. Everybody must work to use the tools we now have available to combat these diseases.

Glossary

Suggested Reading List

References

Index

Abortion The premature expulsion from the uterus of the embryo or a nonliving fetus.
—**Criminal Abortion** An illegal abortion.
—**Spontaneous Abortion** An abortion occurring naturally. Also called Miscarriage.
—**Therapeutic Abortion** An abortion induced to save the life of the mother.
Adolescence The period of life beginning with the appearance of the secondary sex characteristics and terminating with the cessation of physical growth.
Afterbirth The mass, consisting of the placenta and allied membranes, cast from the uterus after the birth of the child.
Amnion The thin, membranous fluid-filled sac surrounding the embryo/fetus.
Ampulla A general term used to designate a flasklike dilation of a tubular structure.
Androgen A term for substances which possess masculinizing activities, such as the testis hormone.
Areola A circular area of different color surrounding a central point.
—**Areola Mammary** The darkened ring surrounding the nipple of the breast.

Blastocyst The modified blastula of mammals.
Blastomere A cell produced during cleavage.
Blastula The usually spherical structure produced by the cleavage of a fertilized ovum, consisting of a single layer of cells surrounding a fluid-filled cavity.

Cervix Neck.

—Cervix Uterus The lower and narrow end of the uterus.

Chancre The primary lesion of syphilis developing at the site of the syphilitic infection and appearing as a small elevated spot on the skin. This erodes into a reddish ulcer covered with a yellowish substance.

Chorion The outermost membrane which serves as a protective and nutritive covering for the embryo/fetus.

Chromosome One of several more or less rod-shaped bodies which appear in the nucleus of a cell at the time of cell division. The chromosomes contain the genes, or hereditary factors, and are constant in number in each species.

Circumcision The removal of all or a part of the prepuce.

Cleavage The cell division of the zygote. The size of the zygote remains unchanged and the cleavage cells, or blastomeres, become smaller and smaller with each division.

Climacteric The group of changes occurring at the end of the reproductive period in the female or accompanying the normal lessening of sexual activity in the male.

Clitoris A small, elongated, erectile body, situated at the anterior part of the vulva; analogous to the penis in the male.

Coitus Sexual union between individuals of the opposite sex.

Colostrum The thin milky fluid secreted by the mammary gland a few days before or after the baby is born.

Corpus Albicans Mass of fibrous scar tissue replacing the corpus luteum.

Corpus Luteum A yellow glandular mass in the ovary formed by an ovarian follicle that has matured and discharged its ovum.

Cryptorchidism A development defect characterized by failure of the testes to descend into the scrotum.

Dysmenorrhea Painful menstruation.

Ectoderm The outermost of the three primary germ layers

of the embryo. From it are developed the epidermis and epidermal tissues such as nails, hair, and glands of the skin, nervous system, and certain parts of the external sense organs.

Ectopic Located away from the normal position.

—Ectopic Pregnancy An extra-uterine pregnancy.

Ejaculatory Duct The canal formed by the union of the vas deferens and excretory duct of the seminal vesicle.

Embryo The early or developing stage of any organism. In the human, the embryo is generally considered to be the developing organism from conception to the end of eight weeks.

Emission A discharge; specifically an involuntary discharge.

—Nocturnal Emission An involuntary discharge of semen during sleep.

Endoderm The innermost of the three primary germ layers of the embryo. From it are derived the lining of the pharynx, respiratory tract (except nose), digestive tract, bladder, and urethra.

Endometrium The mucous lining of the uterus, the thickness and structure of which vary with the phase of the menstrual cycle.

Epididymis The elongated, cordlike structure along the posterior border of the testis. The spermatozoa are stored in the ducts of the epididymis.

Estrogen A term for hormones produced especially in the ovaries and usually characterized by its ability to promote estrus and stimulate the development of the secondary sex characteristics in the female.

Estrus The recurrent, restricted period of sexual receptivity in female mammals marked by intense sexual urge.

Eunuch A male deprived of the testes or external genital organs.

Fallopian Tube The long, slender tube that extends from the upper lateral angle of the uterus to the region of the ovary on the same side. Also called Oviduct and Uterine Tube.

Fertilization The fusion of a spermatozoon with an ovum, starting the development of a zygote.

Fetus The developing young in the human uterus after eight weeks. It is an infant when completely outside the mother's body, even before the cord is cut.

Gamete A mature germ cell (either sperm or egg).

Genital Corpuscles Small nerve endings in the mucous membrane of the genital region.

Genital Swelling An elevation on each side of the primitive phallus (the penis or clitoris before development) from which the scrotum or labia majora develops.

Genital Tubercle A protuberance in the early embryo which becomes the penis or clitoris.

Genitalia The reproductive organs, especially the external ones.

Gestation The period of development from the time of fertilization of the ovum to birth.

Glands of Montgomery Sebaceous glands of the mammary areola.

Glans A small rounded mass or glandlike body.

—**Glans Clitoris** Erectile tissue at the end of the clitoris.

—**Glans Penis** The cap-shaped expansion at the end of the penis.

Gonad A gamete-producing gland; an ovary or testis.

Gonadotropic Hormone Any hormone which has an influence on the gonads.

Gonorrhea A contagious inflamation of the genital mucous membrane transmitted chiefly by coitus.

Graafian Follicle A maturing ovarian follicle, comprising a fluid-filled cavity in which the ovum floats.

Hymen The membranous fold which partially or wholly closes the external opening of the vagina.

Implantation The attachment (and embedding) of the blastocyst to the lining of the uterus.

Interstitial Cells The cells that surround the seminiferous tubules of the testis; believed to furnish the internal secretion of the testis. Also called Leydig Cells.

Labia Majora The elongated folds running downward and backward from the mons pubis.

Labia Minora Small folds between the labia majora and the opening of the vagina.

Labor The function of the female organism by which the fetus is expelled from the uterus to the outside world.

Labor Pains The rhythmic pains of increasing severity and frequency caused by contraction of the uterus at childbirth.

Leydig Cells *See* Interstitial Cells.

Lochia The vaginal discharge that takes place during the first week or two after childbirth.

Mammary Gland One of the compound glands that are characteristic of mammals; modified in the female to secrete milk.

Menarche The beginning of the menstrual function.

Menopause The cessation of menstruation in the human female.

Menstrual Cycle The period of regularly recurring physiological changes in the lining of the uterus which culminate in its shedding (menstruation).

Menstrual Flow The discharge that occurs during menstruation.

Menstruation The periodic uterine bleeding of a nonpregnant woman during her reproductive years.

Mesoderm The middle layer of the three primary germ layers of the embryo, lying between the ectoderm and the endoderm. From the mesoderm are derived connective tissue, bone and cartilage, muscles, blood and blood vessels, kidneys, and sex organs.

Miscarriage *See* Abortion, Spontaneous.

Mons Pubis The rounded fleshy prominence over the symphysis pubis (the juncture of the two pubic bones). Also called Mons Veneris.

Mons Veneris *See* Mons Pubis.

Morula A solid mass of blastomeres formed by the cleavage of the fertilized ovum. This fills all of the space occupied by the ovum before cleavage.

Navel *See* Umbilicus.

Nipple The conic organ which gives outlet to milk from the breast.

Orgasm The crisis of sexual excitement.

Ova (pl.; sing., ovum) The female's reproductive cells. Also called eggs.

Ovarian Follicle The egg and its encasing cells at any stage of its development.

Ovary The female gonad which produces the ova.

Oviduct *See* Fallopian Tube.

Ovulation The discharge of a mature, unimpregnated ovum from the graafian follicle of the ovary.

Ovum *See* Ova.

Penis The male organ of coitus.

Placenta The cakelike organ within the uterus; it establishes communication between the mother and the embryo/fetus by means of the umbilical cord.

Prepuce A covering fold of skin, such as that covering the glans penis.

Progesterone A hormone produced by the corpus luteum to prepare the uterus for the reception and development of the fertilized ovum.

Prostate A gland which in the male surrounds the neck of the bladder and the urethra.

Puberty The time of life when the sex organs mature, the secondary sex characteristics appear, and an individual becomes first capable of reproducing.

Quickening The first recognizable movements of the fetus in the uterus.

Scrotum   The pouch which contains the testes and their accessory organs.

Semen   The thick, whitish secretion of the male's reproductive organs. It is composed of spermatozoa and secretions from the prostate, seminal vesicles, and other glands.

Seminal Vesicle   Either of the paired, saclike pouches attached to the back of the urinary bladder; the duct of each joins the vas deferens to form the ejaculatory duct.

Seminiferous Tubules   The numerous canals within each lobe of the testis. The spermatozoa are formed from the lining of these canals.

Sertoli Cells   *See* Sustentacular Cells.

Smegma   A thick cheesy, ill-smelling secretion found under the prepuce in males and around the clitoris in females.

Sperm   *See* Spermatozoa.

Spermatogenesis   The process of formation of the spermatozoa.

Spermatozoa (pl.; sing., spermatozoon)   The male's mature germ cells. Also called Sperm.

Sterility   The inability to produce offspring; that is, the inability to conceive or induce conception.

Sustentacular Cells   Elongated cells in the tubules of the testes to the ends of which the spermatozoa become attached, apparently for nutrition until the spermatozoa mature. Also called Sertoli Cells.

Syphilis   A contagious venereal disease leading to many structural and skin lesions; transmitted usually by direct sexual contact.

—**Congential Syphilis**   Syphilis existing at birth.

Testicle   The male gonad. This gland produces the spermatozoa and is normally located in the scrotum. Also called Testis.

Testis   *See* Testicle.

Testosterone   The hormone produced by the testes; this hormone functions in the induction and maintenance of male secondary characteristics.

Trophoblast   A layer of ectodermal tissue on the outside of the blastocyst. It attaches to the uterine wall and supplies nutrition to the very early embryo.

Umbilical Cord   The flexible structure connecting the umbilicus with the placenta and giving passage to the umbilical arteries and vein.

Umbilicus   The new tissue formed at the site of attachment of the umbilical cord to the embryo/fetus. Also called Navel.

Urethra   The membranous canal which conveys urine from the bladder to the exterior of the body.

Uterine Tube   *See* Fallopian Tube.

Uterus   The hollow, muscular organ in females which is the abode and place of nourishment of the embryo/fetus. Also called Womb.

Vagina   The canal in the female extending from the vulva to the cervix of the uterus.

Vas Deferens   The excretory duct of the testis which unites with the excretory duct of the seminal vesicle to form the ejaculatory duct.

Venereal Disease   A contagious disease, such as syphilis and gonorrhea, usually acquired in sexual intercourse.

Vestibule   The space or cavity at the entrance to a canal.

—Vestibule Vagina   The space between the labia minora into which the urethra and vagina open.

Villi   Small vascular protusions, especially such protusions from the free surface of a membrane.

—Chorionic Villi   Threadlike projections growing in tufts on the external surface of the chorion.

Vulva   The region of the external genital organs of the female.

Wet Dream   An erotic dream culminating in an orgasm and in the male accompanied by a nocturnal emission.

Womb   *See* Uterus.

Zona Pellucida   The transparent noncellular layer surrounding the morula.

Zygote   The cell resulting from the fusion of two gametes; the fertilized ovum.

SUGGESTED READING LIST

About Syphilis and Gonorrhea. Washington, D. C.: U. S. Dept. of Health, Education, and Welfare. Public Health Service Publication No. 410, 1961.

Accent on You. New York: Tampax Inc., 1966.

Bundesen, Herman N. *Toward Manhood.* Philadephia: J. B. Lippincott Co., 1951.

Burnett, R. Will, and others. *Life Goes On,* 2nd ed. New York: Harcourt, Brace & World, Inc., 1959.

Butterfield, Oliver M. *Sexual Harmony in Marriage.* New York: Emerson Books, Inc., 1953.

Call, Alice L. *Toward Adulthood.* Philadelphia: J. B. Lippincott Co., 1964.

Clendening, Logan. *The Human Body.* New York: Alfred A. Knopf, Inc., 1945.

Cohen, Yehudi A. *Transition from Childhood to Adolescence.* Chicago: Aldine Publishing Co., n.d.

Corner, George W. *Attaining Manhood,* rev. ed. New York: Harper & Row Pubs., 1952.

———. *Attaining Womanhood,* rev. ed. New York: Harper & Row Pubs., 1952.

Crawley, Lawrence Q., and others. *Reproduction, Sex, and Preparation for Marriage.* Englewood Cliffs, N. J.: Prentice-Hall, Inc., 1964.

Crossley, Robert P. "Quints, Anyone? Could It Happen to You?" *Popular Science,* 185 (Sept., 1964), 53–55+.

Dahlberg, Gunnar. "An Explanation of Twins." *Scientific American,* 184 (Jan., 1951), 48–51.

Dickerson, Roy. *Into Manhood.* New York: Association Press, 1954.

Donovan, B. T., and J. J. van der Werff ten Bosch. *Physiology of Puberty.* Baltimore: Williams & Wilkins Co., 1965.

Duvall, Evelyn M. *Love and the Facts of Life.* New York: Association Press, 1963.

————. *Why Wait Till Marriage?* New York: Association Press, 1965.

Eradication of Syphilis. Washington, D. C.: U. S. Dept. of Health, Education, and Welfare. Public Health Service Publication No. 918, 1963.

Flanagan, Geraldine. *The First Nine Months of Life.* New York: Simon and Schuster, Inc., 1962.

Growing Up and Liking It. Milltown, N. J.: Personal Products Co., 1966.

Hilliard, Marion. *A Woman Doctor Looks at Love and Life.* New York: Doubleday & Co., Inc., 1957.

History of V.D. Harrisburg: Commonwealth of Pennsylvania, Dept. of Health, n.d.

Keliher, Alice V. *Life and Growth.* New York: Appleton-Century-Crofts, 1941.

Landers, Ann. *Ann Landers Talks to Teen-agers about Sex.* Englewood Cliffs, N. J.: Prentice-Hall, Inc., 1963.

Levine, Milton, and Jean H. Seligmann. *The Wonder of Life.* New York: Golden Press, Inc., 1952.

Maternity Center Association, ed. *A Baby Is Born.* New York: Grosset & Dunlap, Inc., n.d.

Michelmore, Susan. *Sexual Reproduction.* New York: Doubleday & Co., Inc., 1965.

Moore, John A., and others. *Biological Science: An Inquiry into Life*, rev. ed. New York: Harcourt, Brace & World, Inc., 1963.

National Venereal Disease Control Program. Washington, D. C.: U. S. Dept. of Health, Education, and Welfare. Public Health Service Publication No. 56, 1959.

Newman, Horatio H. "About Twins," *New York Times Magazine*, Nov. 14, 1948, Sec. 6, p. 24.

Oraison, Marc. *Learning to Love: Frank Advice for Young Catholics.* New York: Hawthorn Books, Inc., 1965.

Shultz, Gladys Denny. *It's Time You Knew.* Philadelphia: J. B. Lippincott Co., 1955.

Shultz, Gladys Denny. *Letters to Jane,* rev. ed. Philadelphia: J. B. Lippincott Co., 1960.

Simpson, George G., and others. *Life: An Introduction to Biology,* 2nd ed. New York: Harcourt, Brace & World, Inc., 1965.

Strain, Frances B. *Teen Days: A Book for Boys and Girls.* New York: Appleton Century, 1946.

Strictly for Teenagers. Washington, D. C.: U. S. Dept. of Health, Education, and Welfare. Public Health Service Publication No. 913, 1962.

Sullivan, Walter. "Venereal Disease," *New York Times,* April 5, 1964, Sec. 4, p. 7.

Syphilis: Modern Diagnosis and Management. Washington, D. C.: U. S. Dept. of Health, Education, and Welfare. Public Health Service Publication No. 743, 1961.

Tanner, James M., and Gordon R. Taylor. *Growth.* Morristown, N. J.: Silver Burdett Co., 1965.

Trimbos, C. J. *Healthy Attitudes Towards Love and Sex.* New York: P. J. Kenedy & Sons, 1964.

Very Personally Yours. Neenah, Wis.: Kimberly-Clark Corp., 1961.

REFERENCES

About Syphilis and Gonorrhea. Washington, D. C.: U. S. Dept. of Health, Education, and Welfare. Public Health Service Publication No. 410, 1961.

Arey, Leslie B. *Developmental Anatomy,* 7th ed. Philadelphia: W. B. Saunders Co., 1965.

Basmajian, J. V. *Cates' Primary Anatomy,* 5th ed. Baltimore: Williams & Wilkins Co., 1964.

Berger, Andrew J. *Elementary Human Anatomy.* New York: John Wiley & Sons, Inc., 1964.

Best, Charles H., and Norman B. Taylor. *The Living Body: A Text in Human Physiology,* 4th ed. New York: Holt, Rinehart & Winston, Inc., 1958.

Blood Grouping Anti-Rh and Anti-Human Serums, 6th ed. Chicago: Michael Reese Research Foundation, 1958.

Bray, William E. *Clinical Laboratory Methods,* 6th ed. by John D. Bauer and others. St. Louis: C. V. Mosby Co., 1962.

Carlson, Anton J., and others. *The Machinery of the Body,* 5th ed. Chicago: University of Chicago Press, 1961.

Curtis, Arthur H., and John W. Huffman. *A Textbook of Gynecology,* 6th ed. Philadelphia: W. B. Saunders Co., 1950.

D'Amour, Fred E. *Basic Physiology.* Chicago: University of Chicago Press, 1961.

DeCoursey, Russell Myles. *The Human Organism,* 2nd ed. New York: McGraw-Hill Book Co., 1961.

Eradication of Syphilis. Washington, D. C.: U. S. Dept. of Health, Education, and Welfare. Public Health Service Publication No. 918, 1963.

Francis, Carl C. *The Human Pelvis.* St. Louis: C. V. Mosby Co., 1952.

94

Gray, Henry. *Gray's Anatomy of the Human Body*, 28th ed. by Charles M. Goss. Philadelphia: Lea & Febinger, 1966.

Hegner, Robert. *Parade of the Animal Kingdom*. New York: Macmillan Co., 1946.

History of V.D. Harrisburg: Commonwealth of Pennsylvania, Dept. of Health, n.d.

Hutt, Frederick B. *Animal Genetics*. New York: Ronald Press Co., 1964.

Kimber, Diana Clifford, and others. *Anatomy and Physiology*, 15th ed. New York: Macmillan Co., 1966.

Langdon-Davies, John. *Seeds of Life*. New York: New American Library, Inc., 1955.

National Venereal Disease Control Program. Washington, D. C.: U. S. Dept. of Health, Education, and Welfare. Public Health Service Publication No. 56, 1959.

Oliven, John F. *Sexual Hygiene and Pathology: A Manual for the Physician and the Professions*. Philadelphia: J. B. Lippincott Co., 1965.

Oppenheimer, Ernst, ed. *The Ciba Collection of Medical Illustrations*, Vol. 2, *Reproductive System*. Summit, N. J.: Ciba Pharmaceutical Products, Inc., 1954.

Parsons, Langdon, and Sheldon C. Sommers. *Gynecology*. Philadelphia: W. B. Saunders Co., 1962.

Patten, Bradley M. *Foundations of Embryology*. New York: McGraw-Hill Book Co., 1958.

Rogers, Terence A. *Elementary Human Physiology*. New York: John Wiley & Sons, Inc., 1961.

Sinnott, Edmund W., and others. *Principles of Genetics*, 5th ed. New York: McGraw-Hill Book Co., 1958.

Snyder, Laurence H., and Paul R. David. *The Principles of Heredity*, 5th ed. Boston: D. C. Heath & Co., 1957.

Strictly for Teenagers. Washington, D. C.: U. S. Dept. of Health, Education, and Welfare. Public Health Service Publication No. 913, 1962.

Syphilis: Modern Diagnosis and Management. Washington, D. C.: U. S. Dept. of Health, Education, and Welfare. Public Health Service Publication No. 743, 1961.

Taylor, E. Stewart. *Essentials of Gynecology*, 3rd ed. Philadelphia: Lea & Febinger, 1965.

Tuttle, W. W., and Byron A. Schottelius. *Textbook of Physiology*, 15th ed. St. Louis: C. V. Mosby Co., 1965.

White, Colin, and Grace Wyshak. "Inheritance in Human Dizygotic Twinning," *New England Journal of Medicine*, 271 (Nov. 5, 1964), 1003–5.

Williams, John W. *Obstetrics*, 13th ed. by Nicholson J. Eastman and Louis M. Hellman. New York: Appleton-Century-Crofts, 1966.

Winchester, Albert M. *Genetics*, 3rd ed. Boston: Houghton Mifflin Co., 1966.

Winchester, Albert M., and Harvey B. Lovell. *Zoology*, 3rd ed. Princeton, N. J.: D. Van Nostrand Co., Inc., 1961.

Wolf-Heidegger, Gerhard. *Atlas of Systematic Human Anatomy*. New York: Hafner Publishing Co., Inc., 1962.

Abdominal pregnancy. *See* Pregnancy, ectopic
Abortion, 50
Adolescence, 5
Afterbirth, 55, 56
Amnion: development of, 44
Amniotic sac: rupture of, 53; with fraternal twins, 62; with identical twins, 63; mentioned, 55
Ampulla: of vas deferens, 14; of lactiferous duct, 32
Androgen: secreted by interstitial cells, 12–13; in females, 26
Areola: of breast, 30–31
Aschheim-Zondek test, 49

Birth: defects preventable, 52; onset of labor in, 53; breech, 55; caesarean, 56; premature, 56; physiological adjustments of baby after, 57–60
Blastocyst stage: described, 41–44; mentioned, 63
Blue baby, 59

Body stalk: umbilical cord developed from, 45
Breasts: development of, 30; description of, 30–32; glands of Montgomery of, 31; lactiferous ducts of, 32; starting and maintaining milk secretion of, 32; cessation of milk secretion of, 60
Breech birth, 55

Caesarean section, 56
Castration, 13
Cervix of uterus: connected with vestibule by vagina, 20; dilation of during labor, 53; mentioned, 28, 51, 55
Chancre, 70
Chorion: development of, 44–45; with fraternal twins, 62; with identical twins, 63
Chorionic gonadotropin: produced by placenta, 45; effect of on corpus luteum, 46; mentioned, 49
Chromosomes: in head of sperm, 39; X of egg cell, 65; XY of sperm cell, 65

Cilia: of epididymis, 14; of fallopian tube, 22, 39

Circulatory system: change in after birth, 58–59

Circumcision, 7

Cleavage stage: described, 41; mentioned, 63

Climacteric. *See* Menopause

Clitoris: description of, 19

Colostrum, 32

Conception: possible after menopause, 29; meeting of sperm and egg, 39

Congenital syphilis, 71–72

Corpus albicans, 25

Corpus luteum: development of, 25; produces progesterone, 26, 27, 30, 44, 46, 51; mentioned, 49

Cryptorchidism, 10–11

Digestive system: after birth, 59–60

Ductus arteriosus, 58, 59

Ectoderm: development of, 42, 44; mentioned, 45

Egg: within follicle, 25; fertilized, 26, 27, 41, 44, 63; not fertilized, 26, 27; in multiple birth, 61, 63, 64; mentioned, 3, 22, 24, 39

Ejaculatory duct, 14

Embryo: use of term, 10; development of from zygote, 41; nourishment of, 44–45; position of in uterus, 51–52; development of in multiple birth, 61, 63, 64

Embryonic period: cleavage stage, 41; blastocyst stage, 41–42; growth during, 46

Emission: characteristics of, 15; nocturnal, 15–16

Endoderm: development of, 42; mentioned, 45

Endometrium: description of, 22; influence of hormones on, 26, 27; mentioned, 44, 51

Epididymis: description of, 14; mentioned, 15

Estrogen: in males, 12; secreted by ovaries, 26, 27; influence of breast development of, 30, 32; prevents ovulation, 46; production of during nursing of baby, 60

Estrus cycle of animals, 34–36

Eunuch, 11, 13

Fallopian tubes: description of, 22; mentioned, 24, 41

Fetal period: growth during, 47

Fetus: use of term, 10; nourishment of, 44–45; position of in uterus, 51, 52; in birth, 53–55; cir-

culatory system of, 58;
mentioned, 41, 50
Fimbriae, 22
Follicle-stimulating hor-
mone (FSH), 24, 26, 27
Follicles: present at birth,
24; cycle of ovarian, 24–
26
Foramen ovale, 58–59

Genital corpuscles: of penis, 7; of clitoris, 19
Genital swellings: form
scrotum, 8; form labia
majora, 19
Genital tubercle: forms penis, 6; forms clitoris, 19
Germinal ridges of tissue,
9–10
Glands of Montgomery, 31
Glans: of penis, 6; of clitoris, 19
Gonadotropic hormones,
24, 48
Gonococcus, 72, 73
Gonorrhea: development
of, 72–73; effects of, 73;
diagnosis and treatment
of, 73–74
Graafian follicle, 25, 46

Heartbeat: of fetus, 51–
52; of newborn, 57, 58
Hormones: produced by
hypophysis, 3, 24; effect
of on male, 3–4; effect of
on female, 4; secreted by
interstitial cells, 12; influence of on ovaries, 24;
produced by corpus lu-
teum, 26; and breast
development, 30
Hymen, 20
Hypophysis. *See* Gonado-
tropic hormones; Hor-
mones

Implantation: of blasto-
cyst, 44; position of in
uterus, 51
Inguinal canal, 10
Inguinal hernia, 10
Inner cell mass: division
of, 42; incomplete divi-
sion of possible cause of
Siamese twins, 63; men-
tioned, 45
Interstitial cells: location
of, 11–12
Involution, 56–57

Labia majora: description
of, 18
Labia minora: description
of, 19
Labor: beginning of, 53;
stage of dilation of, 53;
stage of descent of, 53–
54; placental stage of, 55
Lactiferous ducts, 32
Leydig cells. *See* Interstitial cells.
Ligament: broad, 22, 24;
of ovary, 24; suspensory,
24
Lochia, 56–57

Lungs: adjustment of after birth, 57–58

Luteinizing hormone (LH), 24, 25

Luteotropic hormone (LTH), 24, 30, 60. *See also* Prolactin

Mammary glands. *See* Breasts

Mating among humans: more than instinctive act, 36; male's response, 37; female's response, 37–38

Menarche, 26, 27, 29, 30

Menopause: age of, 26; pregnancy possible after, 29

Menstrual cycle: variations in, 26; three phases of, 27–28; and conception, 38; mentioned, 24, 25, 36, 61

Menstruation: description of, 26–29; return of after pregnancy, 57; mentioned, 4

Mesoderm: development of, 44

Miscarriage, 50. *See* Abortion

Mons pubis, 17

Mons veneris, 17

Morula, 41–42

Nervous system: after birth, 60

Nipple, 30, 31, 32

Nocturnal emission. *See* Emission, nocturnal

Octuplets, 61

Ovaries: and broad ligament, 22; development of, 23–24; description of, 24; hormones secreted by, 26; mentioned, 3, 25, 30, 51

Ovulation: rupture of ovarian follicle, 25; end of first phase of menstrual cycle, 27; mentioned, 29, 34, 38, 57, 61

Ovum. *See* Egg

Pelvic girdle, 17

Pelvis: female differs from male, 17; and broad ligament, 22; mentioned, 24, 56

Penis: development of, 6; description of, 6–8

Pituitary. *See* Hypophysis

Placenta: development of 44–45; provides nourishment for embryo / fetus, 45; hormonal activity of, 45–46; with fraternal twins, 61; with identical twins, 63; mentioned, 48, 51, 55, 58, 60

Pregnancy: tests of historical interest for, 48–49; current tests for, 49;

ectopic, 49–50; normal, 50–52; diet during, 51; mentioned, 30, 53, 54, 57

Premature birth, 56

Primary sex characteristics, 4

Progesterone: produced by corpus luteum, 25; effect of, 26; produced by placenta, 26; during pregnancy, 46. *See also* Corpus luteum; Placenta

Prolactin: secreted after puberty, 24; affects development of breast, 30; starts secretion of milk, 32; production of during nursing of baby, 60

Prostate gland: description of, 14–15

Puberty: age of onset of, 4

Quadruplets: frequency and development of, 64

Quickening, 52

Quintuplets: frequency and development of, 64; Dionne, 64

Rh factor, 66–67

Scrotum: description of, 8; development of, 8

Secondary sex characteristics, 3–4

Semen: description of, 15

Seminal vesicle: description of, 14

Seminiferous tubules: description of, 11; mentioned, 15

Septuplets, 61

Sertoli cells, 11

Sex determination, 65–66

Sextuplets, 61

Smegma, 7

Sperm: description of cell, 11; movement of in male, 14; continual supply of, 15; movement of in female reproductive tract, 38–39; mentioned, 3

Sustentacular cells, 11

Symphysis pubis: juncture of two pubic bones, 17

Syphilis: history of, 68–69; description of organism, 69–70; development of, 70–71; effects of, 71; congenital, 71–72; diagnosis and treatment of, 72

Testes: development of, 9–10; description of, 11; mentioned, 3

Testosterone, 12

Treponema pallidum, 69–70

Triplets: frequency of, 63; development of, 63–64

Trophoblast, 44

Tubal pregnancy. *See* Pregnancy, ectopic

Twins: frequency of, 61; development of fraternal, 61–62; development of identical, 63; Siamese, 63; mentioned, 25

Umbilical cord: development of, 45; cutting of, 55; with identical twins, 63

Urethra: of male, 7–8; of female, 20

Uterus: description of, 20–22; movement of egg into, 22; size of during pregnancy, 50; position of embryo / fetus in, 51; shrinkage of after delivery, 56–57; mentioned, 24, 42, 50, 53, 56, 68.

See also Endometrium; Implantation

Vagina: description of, 20; mentioned, 7, 21, 28, 53, 55, 57

Vas deferens: description of, 14; mentioned, 15

Venereal disease: epidemics of, 68; syphilis, 68–72; gonorrhea, 72–74; precautionary guidelines, 74; control of, 74–76

Vernix caseosa, 47

Vestibule, 19–20

Wasserman test, 72

Zona pellucida, 41

Zygote: union of egg and sperm cells makes, 40; mentioned, 41, 63